Morag Macleod

PRESSED
but not
CRUSHED

A True Life Story of Living With Faith
and Locked-In Syndrome

Andrew Davies

with Barbara Davies and Emma Davies

D1313257

PUBLISHING

First published 2015 by Malcolm Down Publishing Ltd
www.malcolmdown.co.uk

British Library Cataloguing in Publication Data

A catalogue record for this book is available from the British
Library

ISBN 978-1-910786-09-3

Authors note: I have tried to recreate events, locales and
conversations from my memories of them. In order to maintain
that anonymity, in some instances I have changed the names
of individuals and places. I may have changed some identifying
characteristics and details such as physical properties,
occupations and places of residence.

Cover Design by Esther Kotetcha.
Image used under licence from aquariagirl1970/Shutterstock.com
Printed in the UK

Contents

We are hard pressed on every side, but not crushed; perplexed, but not in despair; persecuted, but not abandoned; struck down, but not destroyed.
(2 Corinthians 4:8-9)

Foreword

Many people journey through life relatively unscathed, though they may occasionally have a brush with pain or difficulty of some kind or other. After all, that's pretty much what life is like, good times are counterbalanced by bad ones. But there are some people who face tragedy and trauma in such a way that we are left amazed at their fortitude and character. We maybe only meet a few of these people in a lifetime. They experience things we only have nightmares about, and somehow they navigate the stormy waters of their personal circumstances whilst retaining their faith in a good God.

That's probably what the apostle Paul meant when he said, 'But we have this treasure in jars of clay to show that this all-surpassing power is from God and not from us. We are hard pressed on every side, but not crushed; perplexed, but not in despair; persecuted,

but not abandoned; struck down, but not destroyed'
(2 Corinthians 4:7–9). We expect such strength from
a Bible hero like Paul, but maybe not from the people
around us that seem as ordinary as we feel. That is the
kind of strength and faith I have witnessed with Andy
and Emma Davies.

I knew Andy long before the tragedy that has left
him with seemingly impossible limitations. I was
close to a man who lived an active and busy life, and
who discussed with me on many occasions his faith
questions as he was working out what it means to
walk with God in the ordinary and difficult things of
life. I was there to celebrate his wonderful wedding to
Emma and the beginnings of their relationship, and
even to help them as they adjusted to the challenges of
understanding each other. But I will always remember
1 November 2011, the shock and repercussions of that
day and the remarkable love and commitment of both
Andy and Emma's family, as well as numerous friends.

Faith maybe isn't really faith until it's been tested.
Though we each pray for a smooth ride through life,
it is only when the wheels seems to come off that we
discover what (and who) really means most to us. This
book plots that journey thus far for Andy Davies and his
devoted wife, Emma, my dear friends. It tells us all about
things we've often wondered when people are trapped
in a coma and we are left confused as to whether they

are aware of those who sit seemingly passive by the hospital bed. It also tells us that a journey back from the brink of death is paved with enormous challenges. But most of all, it tells us that God has equipped the human spirit with the ability to battle through times of doubt and pain with an indomitable trust in Him.

The story isn't complete yet for Andy and Emma, and the way ahead probably does have more challenges – but isn't that true for all of us? I am sure that as you read this story, you'll be moved and inspired to face your battles with fresh courage. We are all grateful that we can live out our future in the ultimate confidence that the God who began it with us will not abandon us on the way to all that He has promised us.

Stuart Blount
Senior Pastor, Christian Life Centre, Birmingham
Spring 2015

Introduction

This book has been a project which has spanned over two years of the three hardest ones of my life. When I first came out of hospital and set up to be able control my computer, I was desperate to communicate some of my memories and perspectives of my incarceration in the various hospitals. These memories were hitherto imprisoned in my mind; unable to find release in any way. I laid down these memories using my new computer. This has an infra-red box above the screen, which tracks the movement of a reflective sticky spot on my forehead and allows me to move the cursor on the screen with movements of my head. Together with a splint, which I wear to utilise a small flicker of movement in my right thumb, I can click to select what my cursor is pointing to. If I use an on-screen keyboard, I am able to type very slowly. I painstakingly typed my memories one click at a time for hours. With every click of my splint, I felt the burden being lifted from my mind. Over the next year I continued to make more observations and chronicle my life. I was able to send copies of a few chapters to friends and family, and for the first time in two years felt able to communicate freely and say everything I wanted, without interruption or misunderstanding.

I then started university, and with the additional workload this demanded my book project went on hold. When I finished my first year, I returned to those collections of chapters and finished the book that you hold in your hands today.

When I initially expressed an interest in expanding my memoirs into a published book format, I was advised by a few knowledgeable people that I should first identify my audience and decide what message I wanted to communicate.

During this project I have been unable to identify a specific group of people who might want to read this book. However, perhaps my friends and family, Christians facing difficulties, other disabled people searching for hope, and medical professionals wishing to gain some insight, may find it valuable. Writing this book initially was purely a selfish exercise that has evolved into a project wishing to help individuals better understand. I really hope you enjoy reading it as much as I enjoyed writing it.

Andrew Davies
Spring 2015

Chapter 1

Perfect Life?

It was 8 p.m. It was still comfortably warm, with low humidity and a gentle sea breeze. Emma had just gone to the bathroom, before our dinner arrived. We had spent the afternoon and the early evening apart to make the night seem even more special. We had both taken advantage of the spa treatments available and relaxed by the pool. I was alone once more for a few minutes. I looked around at the massive expanse of the Mediterranean and focused on the ship's wake, which stretched to the horizon, and took a sip of my champagne. I spoke to God as naturally as I could without making a sound.

'What's the purpose of my life?' I questioned.

I often used to pray to God, but somehow this seemed different; I don't know whether it was the emotion of the evening or whether there was more of a connection than usual, but I remember feeling His distinct presence. Normally, when there are so many positive distractions filling my mind, I can temporarily forget God, but tonight my spiritual senses were awakened. We were enjoying silver service, eating in Marco Pierre White's restaurant aboard P&O's cruise ship, *Ventura*. This was our first-ever cruise and within a few days we realised why so many people love it. We were staying in what was essentially a five-star, full-board floating hotel. Each day we had a new destination to explore and each night we indulged by watching West End-style shows and eating in a variety of silver service restaurants. It was our second wedding anniversary and we had booked the cruise around this date. I continued sipping champagne, confused as to why I and Emma, who were willing to give so much of ourselves to God, appeared to remain fairly unchallenged, or at least not challenged more than anyone else. Instead we were feeling more and more blessed in everything we did.

Our holiday was also intended to celebrate the end of my first year as Vocational Trainee Advisor. I had been appointed to what was, for me, the perfect job. I remember praying just before my interview that I didn't want the job unless it was God's specific will. I knew I would never cope on my own. Following five years teaching students at the University of Birmingham Dental School, I was appointed as one of the advisors for post-graduate training. This was a huge and unexpected leap in my career. Many people aspire to be a vocational advisor as they become more senior in the dental profession. Candidates are normally in their forties or fifties with numerous postgraduate qualifications. I was the youngest person in the country to have ever held such a position and very underqualified; I assume when I applied there wasn't much interest, and because I was technically qualified I was offered the job, with the implicit understanding that I improve on my non-existent postgraduate qualifications! So, that is how I ended up studying for the PGCE (Postgraduate Certificate in Education) and my Membership of the Joint Dental Faculties in the Royal College of Surgeons simultaneously. Although the job was quite demanding with additional pressures to being a normal dentist, it came with rewards in influence, potential acknowledgement, free education and, of course, a good salary. The salary was probably not as much as someone could earn in practice, but it was in return for doing a job I loved.

As I sat drinking champagne and communicating with God, I thought I heard confirmation that my purpose was to demonstrate how blessed one person can be by having faith in Him. It certainly fitted with how I was feeling just then. So many times in our lives we don't appreciate what we have until we lose it and that certainly was true of me most of the time; but for that moment, on that night, I realised just how much I had and was more than content.

When that moment was over, I would go back to my everyday life, enjoying it but not awestruck by the number of blessings I had. It was just my life and I suppose we are all guilty of accepting our lives as the norm. I don't know how many people feel like this, but it seems whatever we have, somehow to be really content, it feels we need just a little bit more. I know I'm not unique in this: John D. Rockefeller, who tops the rich list of the twentieth century, was allegedly asked, 'How much money would it take for you to be really satisfied?' He replied: 'Just a little bit more.' Even Paul, who wrote a large proportion of the New Testament, said he had 'learned to be content' (Philippians 4:11), which suggests that it didn't come naturally. In regards to career, home life and church life, although I was happy in these, there always seemed to be a drive that said, 'Just a little bit more.' This was a useful drive with regards to my career and earning potential; however, at the time, I didn't fully understand how much that drivenness would assist me in the road that lay ahead. My life until now had seemed to get better and better. I grew up as a happy child in Burscough, a small village in north-west England, with my mum and dad, brother and sister. I was involved with Scouts and enjoyed camping and outdoor events. At school I was fairly average but seemed to be better at maths and science; this was probably following my dad's abilities as a maths and physics teacher. I enjoyed drama and singing and probably, if I'm honest, I craved being the centre of attention. I attended a sixth form college away from all my former friends and wonderfully ended up in a group of people highly motivated for professional careers. Certainly it wasn't 'cool' anymore to not do any work, or at least brag that you hadn't; rather than being embarrassed about getting a high mark, there was competition. It was at this point that I realised I also had the ability for a professional career; I chose dentistry. I had considered medicine but this seemed purely academic; I had always been good with my hands, and dentistry required the perfect combination of academic ability and practical skills.

The University of Birmingham accepted my application. In my first year, I became intensely homesick; this was initially triggered by my bike being stolen, which was also my eighteenth birthday present. I was also increasingly feeling out of my depth academically. I had come from doing A-levels, where I was towards the top of the class, to university where I was average at best but often felt significantly less. My homesickness lasted about a year, during which time my mum and dad encouraged me to just 'keep plodding on'. During this time I probably learned how to choose to do what I thought was right, in this case continuing with uni, whist still feeling wretched. I had to take control over my emotions, which were screaming, 'Give up!' and do whatever I judged to be right, regardless of my feelings. When I returned for my second year, my homesickness had subsided and I was able to focus solely on just getting through university, so that I could realise my ambition of becoming a dentist. On the whole, my time at uni was enjoyable and I made some fantastic friends.

Once I had qualified, I did a probationary year in a small practice in Dudley, and I had remained there as an associate. Over these years, I was quite target-driven; to begin with, my goal was to have a nice car and then again to buy a house, with the ultimate hope of being able to settle down and provide for a family. Emma and I met in April 2007 and quickly got engaged. In July 2008, we were married. Now my ambitions included someone else as well and I wanted to be sure I could provide for our future life together. I had already insured my hands when I qualified, but now I wanted to take out life insurance to pay off our mortgage in the event of me becoming critically ill. After a year of marriage, we moved house to our potentially dream home in Bournville, not only a chocolate-box village but one actually built for the local Cadbury factory.

I enjoyed staying busy and did a number of jobs around the church. I took on responsibility for the church lighting and found my education in mathematics invaluable for understanding the communication and programming system between the console and the lights. I also enjoyed helping with the Teen Challenge ministry, which tried to befriend and support people with life-controlling addictions. We used to drive a bus into town and provide a mobile café where people could have a drink and chat. This was another time when I used to contrast my life and upbringing with the life some others contended with, and it would always make me appreciate even more what I had.

At about the same time, Emma and I had been asked to start a young adults group in our church. Before we were married, I had been a youth leader. Now many of the youth were young adults, and so we were able to continue sharing life with them. Inevitably, there were some difficulties, but generally it was really great. It was a time when Emma and I could feel just a bit younger than our years, and really care for some individuals; we witnessed lives completely changing quite rapidly.

That evening on the cruise ship, talking with God was a moment when I was content with everything I had materially and my various achievements and commitments. Our blessings were not simply worldly but seemed to influence every part of our life, and we felt valued by being part of other people's lives. I didn't realise at the time that things would descend to the depths that they did; I could only be excited about the future continuing to get better and better.

Chapter 2

The Stroke

- by Barbara

> Even youths grow tired and weary,
> and young men stumble and fall;
> but those who hope in the LORD
> will renew their strength.
> They will soar on wings like eagles;
> they will run and not grow weary,
> they will walk and not be faint.
> (Isaiah 40:30,31)

My Bible reading for that morning was Isaiah 40 and the words of the last two verses were so powerful. Andy, who was young and 'stumbling', was clearly very frightened by the severe pain in his head and neck and the tingling in his left arm and fingers. As an experienced dentist and medically trained, he realised his symptoms indicated something was seriously wrong but couldn't understand why a CT scan showed no abnormalities. He had been sent home at midnight and told to ring for an 'urgent' appointment for an MRI scan – 'urgent' meaning within seven days.

At 9 p.m. Emma rang to say Andy was back in A&E with his symptoms worsening and was to be kept in for 'observation'. Looking back at my reading I was comforted by the words, 'those who hope in the LORD will renew their strength'. Andy would be alright; he had put his trust in Jesus as a little boy. Surely the Lord was with him? He was a regular at Sunday school, youth fellowship and worship at the local Methodist church. He enjoyed drama and music, taking part in every production at church, high school and college. He loved outdoor, adventurous activities with the Scouts and later as an adult, a keen climber, mountaineer and skier.

In 2002, he qualified as a dentist at Birmingham University. Since then he had worked for the NHS in general dental practice and a drop-in centre. He was currently working as a clinical lecturer, a postgraduate trainer and an advisor for training (the youngest person in the country to hold such a post), an intelligent, dedicated health professional.

In 2008, he married Emma, his beautiful soul-mate, who worked alongside him through the church with young people, many of whom were facing problems and difficulties in their lives. We believed at the time that God had great plans for them as a couple to bring the message of hope in Jesus and God's love to those around them. We could never have imagined what that would mean in reality.

At 3 a.m. on Tuesday, 1 November my husband, Trevor, and I were woken by a call from Emma; Andy's condition had deteriorated, his face drooping and his speech slurred. It could possibly be a dissected artery. We needed to get to Birmingham, and quickly, but practicalities needed to be addressed and telephone calls made. Andy's brother, Paul, and sister, Tina, needed to know. Despite living hundreds of miles apart, the three children were very close; we called them immediately. Tina was already awake with four-month-old Jake, and very concerned, asked us to keep her updated as she couldn't leave her children; Paul got in his car and headed to Birmingham. We had to break the news to Trevor's mum, eighty-nine years old and recently widowed, who was living next door. We were responsible for her care, but our dear friend Dorothy was coming to look after her. As we left for Birmingham, Mum and Dot were praying together for Andy, Emma and us in our travels. We sent messages to as many as possible, to the family, friends and our prayer partners at church: 'Please pray for Andy.'

With an overnight bag packed, we set off to Birmingham and arrived at the hospital. Emma and Paul were waiting outside the Clinical Decisions Unit to meet us; Paul had been told Andy had suffered a small stroke but it was thought the 'event' was complete. Andy had been taken upstairs for the long overdue MRI scan to assess the damage to his brain. He was brought back to the unit on a trolley.

'Hi, Mum,' he said, and he seemed fine, but once we were alone Andy told us of his fear – 'I mustn't have another one [stroke]' and confusion – 'I don't know what's happening'. Emma was exhausted after three horrific days and nights of anxiety, taking Andy to A&E three times and spending the previous night at his side in hospital. She had begged the A&E staff to listen to Andy; with his medical background he knew his condition needed urgent treatment.

The next hours were a blur, staff and patients coming and going and no one to talk to us and tell us what was happening. The four of us took it in turn to sit with Andy as he anxiously pulled at the lifeless left side of his face and limbs, waiting to be admitted to the stroke unit. Andy's condition did seem to have stabilised so Trevor, Paul and I went to Andy and Emma's home in Bournville; Emma wouldn't leave until Andy was safely moved upstairs to 411, saying she would come home at the end of visiting time. A very good friend, Harry (Harriet) would be coming to be with Emma and see Andy on the ward.

Sitting in Andy and Emma's home, feeling numbed

and helpless, we waited for news, fully expecting Emma to call and say Andy was settled and she would be coming back soon. When the phone did ring it was Harry using Emma's phone and so we knew the news was not good. Andy's condition was deteriorating; the doctors were with him; we would get a call as soon as there was news.

Ten minutes later, Harry called again. It was the phone call we most dreaded: 'I think you should all get here as quickly as possible. I'll meet you at the main entrance.' We had never before experienced such fear as we drove to the hospital in shocked silence, ran frantically through the building and up four flights of stairs. We had no thoughts of anything except to get to our precious child.

Andy lay lifeless, his head lolling to the left, his voice silent. His eyes stared pleadingly at us but there were only a few moments to kiss him and reassure him before we were asked to leave and wait in a small room as Andy was being moved to the High Dependency Unit up the corridor. We waited with Emma, Harry and Pastor Stuart from Andy and Emma's church and we prayed and prayed and waited and waited.

Eventually, it seemed like an eternity, a doctor came to us. 'Good news! The drug we have given Andy is working – he is showing signs of responding – moving his right arm and speaking.' We were told we could see Andy before they moved him to the Critical Care Unit where he could be monitored and treated more effectively. We thought the worst was over but as Trevor and I went into the darkened ward we watched, horrified, as a great seizure took hold of Andy, his head thrown back as he fought for breath. The doctor at his side instantly opened his airway and called for help; nurses curtained off the bed and we were left terrified, clinging to each other, helpless. We stumbled back to the others in the waiting room and we all prayed; prayed that Andy's life would be spared, prayed for a healing miracle.

Andy was to be moved immediately to the Critical Care Unit where he was to be given full life support and twenty-four hour, one-to-one nursing care. Andy was alive but only just. Whatever the cause of Andy's illness, his whole body had ceased to function. His heart, lungs, blood pressure and body temperature were out of control; the machinery, drugs and vigilant nursing care were keeping Andy's body alive. We were given a few minutes to be with him before he was heavily sedated. Taking it in turn at his bedside, we assured him of our love and God's love for him and that we would be praying constantly. We left him there, trusting in God's loving care and the skill of the medical team.

The following days were all one long nightmare. Unable to sleep, eat, read or even talk, the whole family existed together, each consumed by shock, unutterable anguish and despair. Too traumatised to do anything else, we focused on Andy, taking it in turn to sit by his side, to comfort and reassure and support Emma, his brave, courageous wife. Our wordless prayers were expressed in tears and aching hearts.

We were all asked to attend a meeting with the doctors at 1 p.m. Dreading what this meant, we could never have imagined the horror of what we were to be told. As I passed Andy's bed, I looked and saw him staring, wide-eyed and motionless. The pain was almost intolerable but I couldn't stop and hold my son or comfort him, I had to pass by, move on to the meeting room.

Sat in a soulless, sparsely furnished room, around a table set with only a box of tissues, our little family sat with a group of medical staff. The senior consultant introduced himself and his colleagues and dropped his head as he gave us the clinical diagnosis of Andy's condition. The exact words washed over us and became lost, but the impact of those words is as vivid to me now as when they were spoken. Here is a paraphrase of what he said:

'Andy has had a major stroke in the brain stem, the control centre of the brain. This has left him with Locked-in syndrome which means his entire body has shut down, but the cognitive part of his brain is undamaged.

He retains all his knowledge, understanding and intellect; his personality and character are unchanged and he knows exactly what has happened. His condition is critical and, if he survives, the Locked-in syndrome means he is unlikely to be able to live any form of independent life again, totally dependent on others for everything. In which case Andy may not wish to go on...'

The stunned silence was broken by the wail of anguish which consumed Emma, as her body was wracked with tears and uncontrollable pain.

At this point I felt the presence of God's Spirit, speaking to me, reassuring me and prompting me to speak.

'We hear what you are saying but we do not accept this. We are Christians, we believe in God, who created this universe, this planet, who is far greater and more powerful than we can ever imagine. God who created all this can heal a tiny piece of damaged brain! "What is humanly impossible is possible for God" [Luke 18:27, GNT].'

Paul asked questions; Tina, who had been able to come now, cried silent tears, staring through the window on a world that had changed forever. Emma's anguish turned to anger as she relived the nightmare of the repeated visits to A&E and requests for someone to listen to Andy who was an experienced, knowledgeable dentist and medic and knew something was seriously wrong. The consultant asked if she wished to make a formal complaint. Emma declined, not wishing to get any individual into trouble, but did ask that Andy's visits to A&E were investigated, with weekend admissions and services reviewed.

We left the room. Emma went back to Andy and I made my way home to break the news to Trevor, who had been looking after our grandsons. Pastor Stuart came to the house to be with us as I recounted what the doctors had said. Stuart's immediate response was to pray. His prayer was the most powerful and heartfelt I have ever experienced, asking God to raise up Andy, that all the tubes and cables be thrown aside; that Andy be fully healed and his life restored. Again the presence of God and the grace of Jesus settled on us; we were strengthened and comforted in our hour of greatest need.

The next few days are a confused memory of people coming and going, meetings, and above all, waiting. Waiting for hours to be allowed in to see Andy, to give him all the love and encouragement we could, and reassuring him that God was with him. We were told that Andy could hear us, but the severity of the trauma he had suffered combined with heavy sedation would mean his responses would be limited. But God had given us all a lifeline to be able to communicate with Andy. He could blink his eyes to answer questions: once for yes, twice for no.

Pastor Stuart asked, 'Andy, we're going to fight for you; are you going to fight, Andy?" The response was a very strong, single blink. The medical team continually talked to Andy as they adjusted the many tubes, cables and life support systems, and he in turn was able to communicate which drug he felt he needed to manage pain or sedation. Using the blinking response we were able to ask what he wanted or needed and what he wanted us to do. As his sedation was reduced, he was able to remain alert and respond but within minutes the alarms on the monitors would warn that his heart rate, respiration and blood pressure were racing out of control and he needed to rest and sleep again. Very often we would simply sing and pray quietly as he rested. We felt so frightened and helpless but also so thankful for each day we had with Andy; he was still with us, he was still fighting.

The most amazing and inspiring times were when we had the privilege of visiting with Emma. Andy's eyes would fill with life and adoration as he 'spoke' of his love for his beautiful wife, using every ounce of strength he had to look into her eyes. Emma in turn smiled, cheerfully reassuring him of her love and the healing power of God at work in their lives. The obvious love and devotion between Andy and Emma was a constant source of inspiration, especially for fellow patients and their relatives. We were privileged to be able to testify to the faithfulness of God and healing power through Jesus as we were asked many times how Andy and Emma could be so positive in the face of such adversity. Very soon Emma began helping with nursing care, removing excess saliva, caused by the ventilator in his mouth, with an aspirator and supporting his head with a cushion of towels as it rolled lifelessly on to his left shoulder. She was doing everything she could to help and comfort him, never once succumbing to tears or expressing her own pain, either with Andy or anyone else, never once complaining or seeking comfort for herself; such a remarkable young woman. We count ourselves truly blessed that the Lord brought Emma and Andy together and give thanks each day for giving us a wonderful, second daughter.

Yet another meeting was convened with the medical team, this time to discuss the way forward in treating Andy. Even at this point we were told that there was nothing which could be done to 'cure' him. The damage to the brainstem was irrevocable and the severity of the stroke had left Andy's entire body paralysed, but he was able to feel everything, all the pain, all the discomfort and all the mental anguish – but unable to even tell anyone. His vital functions were being managed by machines; machines keeping him alive. It was highly unlikely Andy would ever be able to live an independent life, and in the light of this he may not wish to live...

No way! This was not our decision to make, they should ask Andy, but once again we explained that Andy was very strong, physically, mentally and spiritually. As Christians we believed in God and that nothing is impossible for Him. Would Andy want to have a tracheostomy – a tube inserted directly into his windpipe to aid breathing and deliver extra oxygen directly to his lungs? To be fed via a nasal-gastric tube? Yes! Yes! Yes! Use all your skills and expertise to save Andy!

The next few days were almost dreamlike, spending hours at the hospital or in Bournville. Tina, desperate to be near her brother, made the difficult decision to return home to London with the little ones; this was not the place for a three-year-old and a baby! We had to return to Lancashire to pack suitcases and prepare to stay in Birmingham for as long as necessary. Paul similarly prepared to commute between Lancashire and Birmingham. Friends provided ready-cooked meals, lifts to and from hospital and many strong shoulders to lean on. A friend also dropped a small paperback book through the letterbox: *Running Free: Breaking out of Locked-in Syndrome* (Accent Press, 2011) in which Kate Allatt tells the story of her amazing recovery from a brainstem stroke and Locked-in syndrome. Hungrily, I read Kate's story and the parallels with Andy's story were incredible. The book explained so much about this devastating illness which, until that week, I had never even heard of, and gave us so much understanding of what Andy was going through. This was no coincidence; Kate had recovered and written her book only a few months earlier! In our darkest hour God sent us this message of hope in a very real and irrefutable way, and also gave us the understanding we needed to help Andy in a practical way. God's timing is perfect.

Chapter 3

Hospital: Part 1

So that is how it happened. I was thirty-three, a general dentist and advisor for postgraduate training, and overnight became worse than a baby. I say 'worse' because at least a baby can cry out for help and wriggle if they are uncomfortable, whereas I was lying motionless, unable to make a noise or even turn my head, life in tatters and dreams destroyed.

It seemed my nightmare was triggered by a series of events which started with a fairly innocuous visit to the GP. I had been suffering with unrelenting headaches and pain in my neck for around four weeks. The pain was not severe but constant, persisting night and day and non-respondent to painkillers. Frustrated, I lay there early one Saturday morning, unable to sleep, and decided I had to do something. Leaving Emma in bed, I took myself to the local GP walk-in centre. This really was a last resort; I wasn't one for going to the GP on a whim.

On presentation, the GP felt that the pain in my neck was muscular in its cause, with the headaches being secondary. She referred me to see a private osteopath, one that she had used herself, and I went to see him about ten days later. After his manipulation, the headaches temporarily eased, but the throbbing pain in my neck persisted.

With the painkillers still not working, I was keen to be seen by the osteopath again to have some sort of relief, even if it were only temporary. The earliest that he could see me was a whole week later, so I visited his clinic on the following Friday. Again my neck was manipulated. This time the treatment had no effect on the pain but worryingly, when I returned home that evening, I felt dizzy and nauseous. I immediately emailed the osteopath and he responded promptly, indicating that he was concerned and suggested seeing me at home the following evening. On the Saturday, we were having friends over for dinner and when we had retired to the lounge, the osteopath arrived. He manipulated my neck one last time but immediately the dizziness and nausea returned. Worried, he said that I needed to go straight to A&E, not giving any suggestion of what it might be at this point.

On initial presentation at A&E, in my own professional judgement, I knew something was wrong and even the triage nurse saw me unable to walk normally. However, the doctors assured me I was fine and sent me home. The next night I attended again with worsening symptoms and they explained I really needed an MRI but had to wait until during the week; their solution was to just give me a CT scan there and then, which in turn came with false reassurances that everything was OK so that whatever was causing the symptoms couldn't be serious. After the CT scan, they sent me away again and told me to come back for a MRI, which could take up to a week to arrange.

By the third day, the Monday, I was intermittently going deaf and Emma persuaded me to go back again to A&E. With it not being a weekend, and there being a more qualified doctor on shift, the symptoms were finally diagnosed as something more serious and I was admitted to the Clinical Decision Unit. That night I had the first part of the stroke; I had lost movement down my left side and my face had drooped. The doctors downplayed the severity of the stroke and so I never imagined what would happen next. I continued to lie in CDU with apparently nothing happening until I went for the MRI scan at 5 p.m. on the Tuesday. It was that night that the stroke took full effect and I became locked in.

I remember when I was having the stroke the doctors wanted to intubate but while they waited for a specialist to arrive, I was choking on my tongue. I tried with what little vigour I had left to pull my tongue out of my mouth, but the nurse thought I was trying to grab my oxygen mask and attempted to restrain me. Although I was losing force in my arm, I was aware I still had enough strength for a moment to overpower the nurse and clear my airway. With one determined grab, the sort that can only be due to self-preservation, I lifted my hand, reached inside my mouth, hooked my finger around my tongue and gasped for breath. Then I must have blacked out.

The next time I specifically remember was five days later when the hospital chaplain came to see me. I know this because he told me it was the morning after bonfire night. Knowing who he was, he must have come to my bed during the last few days, probably with my family. Whenever people came to see me I would get a moment of clarity before my blood pressure and heart rate increased and I would return into the continuous nightmare. One of these times was when one of Emma's friends, Elaine, visited when she was on duty; she was an intensive care nurse. She gently said, 'God moves in mysterious ways.' I longed to be able to communicate my tremendous pain and elicit some help to relieve it, but I couldn't even turn my face towards her, let alone demonstrate I had heard and understood who she was. For weeks after, I was desperate to communicate to Emma that her friend had been to see me and, as I became proficient in using my blink chart, I could vaguely describe the nurse to Emma, so that she could confirm she knew who she was. Elaine came to visit me when I came home and was shocked when I recollected my memories of that initial meeting; it is extremely unusual for patients who are heavily sedated to remember anything.

During another of these clear moments I remember Pastor Stuart asking me if I wanted to fight on and to blink once if I did. I gave a single strong blink. On a different visit, I remember Emma's mum looking into my eyes and saying I had been a good husband to their daughter. I also recall seeing friends come in and break down at the sight of me and all the tubes keeping me alive.

I did have some other moments of lucidity. I remember being sedated many times. Not aware of what was happening, I would just become really calm and sleepy and drift away in seconds. On one occasion, I remember thinking I was finally being 'put down'. I think I was resigned to such a fate and so I wasn't panicked. Another time, I had the odd sensation that I was clasping tightly my Mercedes keys in one hand and my wedding band in the other. Panicked that I would lose them, I kept wishing that Paul would retrieve the keys and that Emma would come to the rescue of the wedding ring. Emma has since joked that the wedding band wouldn't have been much use to her and she would have much preferred the Mercedes' keys!

One day I kept confusing my dream and the reality in that I truly believed I had been healed but kept having nightmares that I was unable to move in my bed. After what seemed like ages, I realised I had mixed up dream and reality and what I thought was the nightmare was what was really happening. Realising there were two realities, I had to actively choose to wake myself up and accept the truth that I was in bed, paralysed. This was particularly poignant; I often wonder what the significance, if any, there would have been in choosing to remain in my dream. That same day, I was being cared for by a nurse and she asked me if I would mind if she suggested to her superior that she came back on her next shift and continued to care for me. I blinked once to signal my agreement. There was quite a bond formed between myself and that nurse. I guess because I was so vulnerable and felt safe with her looking after me.

It seems strange to talk about pleasure during such a traumatic time, but three times a day I would have medicines injected down my nasal-gastric tube, with water. It was always cool and, although I couldn't taste the water, I would be able to feel the refreshing effect of it passing down my throat and cooling my stomach. A week after the stroke, the tubes keeping me alive were replaced by a tracheostomy (a hole in my neck with a tube coming out, as Emma described it). I was moved out of the Intensive Therapy Unit (ITU) and transferred onto a high dependency bay of the stroke unit. I was still being observed closely with there being a nurse stationed to watch me and the three other very poorly patients sharing my bay. My life was still in a balance and Emma has since told me of the alarming conversations that she shared with the medical team, warning her that things remained touch and go and reiterating statistics, such as 90 per cent of all patients with brainstem strokes don't make it past the first four months. Despite this, any advice given by doctors was textbook-based; I was effectively their guinea pig as none of the doctors had treated someone with Locked-in syndrome before. I was still connected to lots of machines, but now they were just monitoring me rather than actively keeping me alive. These would alarm sporadically but so would the machines connected to my comrades so I would wake up with an alarm going, never knowing if it was mine. The person in the bed opposite obviously had a naturally low oxygen saturation and therefore his alarm was constantly sounding; knowing this, the nurses would just ignore it! It was always easier in the day when I had visitors there because at least they could turn mine off, but at night I would lay awake to the sound of the continuous droning, just staring up at the ceiling.

Having my tracheostomy fitted meant that I no longer sported the tube from the ventilator, which also worked to prise my mouth open. It became quickly apparent that I was unable to open my mouth; my intense spasms were causing my teeth to clench and clamp down on my tongue. I was left in excruciating pain so my spasms would rocket all the more and the vicious pain cycle would be exacerbated, leaving my blood pressure and heart rate in disarray. I remember my mum trying to calm me down and once again I must have been sedated because I recall being amazed that just a few words from Mum allowed my jaw to relax and I fell asleep quickly. As the sedation wore off, my spasms would return, which would fuel the vicious pain cycle once more. This was, of course, a real concern to the professionals, who were worried that I would end up biting off part of my tongue. The consultant suggested injecting with Botox to paralyse my jaw muscles, but that this may impact on any recovery of my speech and eating functions. It was decided that the speech therapist try regular massaging of my facial muscles first to see if this had any effect. To all our relief, the gentler option seemed to do the trick and my jaw became looser.

On the morning of 22 November, three weeks after my stroke, Emma arrived and was immediately greeted by a tearful speech and language therapist, desperate to share with her the good news. During my therapy session that morning there had been a number of firsts; I had managed to open and close my mouth on command and had taken some sips of water. My eye movement had also improved; I was able to track her finger from left to right and had even managed to turn my head, only half a turn, but it meant that I could voluntarily relieve the pressure from my left ear, which had already developed a nasty pressure sore. We were all ecstatic. Emma immediately updated the blog about me that had been set up, to let others know the good news. This was significant progress; Kate Allatt, who went on to make a full recovery from Locked-in syndrome, was nil by mouth for the first seven months. It was about three weeks after moving to the stroke ward that my times of consciousness increasingly coalesced and I could enjoy a long time of lucidity. I began to meaningfully communicate with my family, using my new means of communication – my blink chart. I still used to sleep for long periods during the day, especially when people visited. I was afraid of dying, so often I found it difficult to sleep at night. However, I felt calmer during visiting times, somehow believing I wouldn't die if someone else was there. Drifting off was mistaken for me not really being bothered about visitors because I was choosing to blank them and getting some rest instead.

During this period, however, I had incredible faith a lot of the time. If someone had asked me to blink to answer questions, they would often get my answer wrong and do the exact opposite. My faith, as it was then, allowed me to believe that my opinion was probably wrong and that God was just overruling my decisions for my own good. So, I was relaxed about people not understanding me, feeling I was better in God's hands anyway. With my faith robust, almost bullish, I was confident for my healing; it was just a case of keeping my mind strong for a few months while I was suffering the worst. I even used to pray for patients next to me for courage to cope with chronic diseases such as diabetes because, after all, I was getting better whereas they were suffering with an ongoing condition. I had had many reassurances that I would be healed, not necessarily miraculously but gradually, over time. The scripture in Isaiah kept appearing again and again. I felt God was speaking to me through many cards, prayers, specific words people thought were relevant to me, and podcasts:

Even youths grow tired and weary and young men stumble and fall; but those who hope in the LORD will renew their strength. They will soar on wings like eagles; they will run and not grow weary, they will walk and not be faint. (Isaiah 40:30,31)

Conversely, there were occasions where I would

lose faith, seriously fearing for my life. I remember spelling out to my friends, Harry and Dan, 'I AM NOT READY TO DIE.' Apart from these panic attacks and severe collapses of faith, I was quite confident that I would be fine, despite people dying all around me. One night I woke up to the voice of an Automatic External Defibrillator (AED) telling the operator there was no need for a shock; I knew this meant the patient was fine or their heart had stopped completely. I saw the body wheeled out; this was the first of many deaths. There was a lot of death on the stroke ward. I assume there was on ITU as well but I wasn't aware enough to notice. It seemed every few days someone would pass away. I began to recognise the signs of someone deteriorating before the nurses would move them into a private room; this was often an indicator that their demise was imminent. However, sometimes even the nurses failed to predict their patients' fate so someone just yards away from me would pass away whilst I was looking on impotently.

Chapter 4

Hospital: Part 2

Although it was implicitly understood that I was fully cognitive, objective tests had to be done to confirm this. On one occasion, I had to prove my cognition to be able to release the funds from my insurance to Emma. Emma was increasingly becoming overdrawn, whereas my bank account contained thousands from my insurance payments but no one could access them. They used to ask me if I knew where I was, who they were, and I would have to blink when they gave me the correct answer. It seemed really silly to confirm I still knew basic buildings and job roles. It was still an issue of pride that I knew I was still providing for Emma in my current state, but all the questions, which could have been answered by a five-year-old, didn't really adequately demonstrate my level of understanding. I just wished I could have communicated my password for my internet banking, which was still stored securely in my head.

During these initial weeks I became a bit more conscious. One of my basic functions that I was still unable to regulate was my body temperature. Every night when Emma or my family visited, I was covered in sweat and burning up. They would fill examination gloves with ice and place them around my body to cool me down. One night a nurse noticed I was smouldering, so she kindly offered to give me a wash before I went to sleep to make me more comfortable. She was humming a Christian worship song called 'Revelation Song' so I knew she was a believer. Months later when I was able to communicate that I was also a Christian, she used to make time each day to come to my bed and read me my calendar which gave a different Christian thought for each day. It turned out she was a senior nurse, known as a sister, and was therefore in charge of a number of staff delivering my care. She was always bubbly and lively and seemed to have the respect and affection of all those she worked with.

At around the time that I became conscious for most of the day, about a month after the stroke, Nathan came onto the ward. Nathan was a Christian, who attended our sister church in the same suburb of Birmingham. I looked across and thought what I saw was a forty- or fifty-something man being wheeled onto the ward with his wife. I later learned the lady he arrived with was his mother and that in fact Nathan was about my age; this came as a shock because I was, until then, the youngest person by far on the stroke ward. When his wife came to see him that evening, it caused me all sorts of confusion. Looking at her through my blurred vision, I saw a young, blonde female and instantly assumed it was Emma, becoming baffled that she had ignored me and had gone straight to the guy opposite. (My eye muscles had been paralysed, which made it difficult to focus.) That night Nathan's father and father-in-law were at his side and they were praying. I couldn't really turn my head to see properly or hear what they were saying. After a while they came over to my bed and introduced themselves as Elim Pentecostal Church pastors. They had heard about me because Stuart had sent around an urgent email requesting prayer when I first became ill; now they asked if they could pray for me in person. I, of course, agreed.

Having Nathan on the ward was quite reassuring even though I couldn't talk to him. One day I was listening to Christian music on my iPod dock and there were shouts of approval from Nathan. Whenever one of our friends came to visit, they would often spend a bit of time with each of us. I remember Nathan's blood pressure being dangerously high and this gave me a focus for my prayer. This was, in fact, helpful for me as I found it easier to focus on praying for someone else. He also had constant hiccups at night so I would wake up and once again be reminded to pray. Thankfully, Nathan's stroke was minor in comparison to mine and he was able to go home a few weeks later. We remain friends.

By mid-December, my tracheostomy was removed. Having the tracheostomy out meant that I could also begin to speak some words. This was a massive breakthrough. Not being able to speak was the most debilitating part of my condition. At this stage I mainly practised speech during therapy sessions and still relied on my blink chart to communicate because most words were far from intelligible (my breathing was significantly affected so I struggled to produce sounds and this was compounded by the fact that my soft palate had also been paralysed, meaning that there was a lot of nasal escape of breath). At first I could only pronounce vowel sounds because they don't require much lip movement and nasal sounds like m and n, meaning that Emma was quite easy to articulate. My speech and language therapist joked it was a good job my wife wasn't called Veronica. My no and yes could only be distinguished by looking at the shape I was trying to form with my lips; they didn't really sound any different. I also began to eat small amounts of soft food and drink thickened fluids. I relied mainly on my nasal-gastric feed at this point for the majority of my calories, around 3,000 a day; despite this, I continued to lose weight because my body was expending so much energy in the healing process.

By Christmas, I was conscious during the whole day and attended therapy whenever I could; however, this was when my frustration really set in. Because of the damage to my brainstem, many of my body's natural functions had stopped working – for example, my breathing and my heart rate – but my ability to experience emotions remained very much intact, although they seemed intensely heightened. My feelings stampeded from dismay to anger and back. My anger became more entrenched and stemmed from my inability to communicate my needs unless my family was present to use my communication board and translate these to those giving care. Apart from the few therapy staff, who had learned my new language, carers guessed what I needed. Then, instead of confirming, they would just assume I had agreed and treat me how they thought was appropriate.

One day, my leg was spasming straight and crushing my toes and so I cried out in pain. Without question, I was given codeine (a painkiller) and diazepam (a sedative) down my nasal-gastric tube and told to wait for the painkillers to work before they would give me a wash. They didn't look to see what was causing the pain, and ignored my crying for fifteen minutes while I waited for the diazepam to reduce my spasms. Similarly, one night I woke up lying on my arm and cried out to get attention. A health care assistant came but thought I was just lonely. I tried to say 'ow' so she knew I needed help; eventually she understood and went to get a nurse. He was ages, but came back with painkillers. I obviously refused; I just needed my hand releasing. Exasperated, he said if I was in pain but refused painkillers, there was nothing he could do; he changed my pad and released my hand in the process. As I lay there recovering, I could hear the carer gossiping about me.

I would often slip down the bed so I would be lying almost flat with my neck bent up at ninety degrees when the bed was sat up. Time and time again I would be given my food in this slumped position. If I coughed, my food would get taken away because I wasn't coping. One morning I was having my breakfast in my usual slumped position when I coughed and, knowing what was coming, I burst into tears. Unable to see what was wrong with me, the nurses got my physio, Claire, who had learned my communication. She took one look at me and said, 'He can't eat like that! He's probably upset because he's slumped.' Despite these frequent misunderstandings, my relationships with the more caring members of the care staff and all of the therapy team were very good.

Although I could feel a spectrum of emotions, my ability to moderate them was often compromised. This would cause me to sometimes cry like a baby but more often laugh uncontrollably. Once my bladder was spasming, causing me lots of pain, and I requested to see the doctor. The doctor came when my friend Pastor Stuart was visiting me and began to ask me about my bowel movement. I was very embarrassed and started to laugh, then Stuart joined in. The doctor was very embarrassed too and didn't know how to cope with me and Stuart laughing! Another time two people from my old youth group came to see me. They left a note by my bed saying my favourite Bible passage was Leviticus 18:23 (about having sex with animals) and I liked people to read it to me. A further time Mum gave me neat cordial thinking it was already diluted. I still couldn't tell her and had to drink it.

By the end of December, nearly two months after the stroke, my therapy sessions also started becoming more dynamic. I was able to be hoisted out of bed and into a normal chair or my wheelchair. My occupational therapist felt that I was now ready to be taken off the ward to get some fresh air outside. This would need to be managed carefully and I would need to remain connected to the pulse oximetre to monitor my oxygen saturation. It was a crisp, cold morning but the sky was clear and the sun was so bright that my eyes were locked in a squinting gaze. I hadn't realised how stale the air was on the ward until I got outside; it felt as if I were discovering fresh air for the first time. There were also the odd sensations which overloaded my senses, like the gentle breeze and the warmth of the sun on my face; I had forgotten such simplicities.

By this time the doctors said that I was stable enough to move to a rehabilitation unit of some description but needed to be free from the nasal-gastric tube before they could refer me. With me still needing so many calories, they felt that a tube going straight into my stomach, a percutaneous endoscopic gastrostomy (PEG) feed, should be fitted to supplement what I was already taking orally. I was booked in for the operation for the following week so my blood-thinning medicines were stopped. Thankfully, the head of speech and language services heard about these plans and insisted that we persist with soft food orally; I would surely be able to cope with taking all food by mouth if I was given just a bit more time. She worked hard with me and I was weaned off all food through my nasal-gastric tube. In early January, I finally had the tube removed without having to have a PEG fitted.

My physiotherapists had been working hard on me using the tilt table with the aim of getting me in an upright position; something much more complex than one would think. Having been lying down for months, there was concern that my blood pressure would become dangerously low if I did this too quickly. Each session, I would be hoisted onto the table and tilted to a new increment, whilst my heart rate and blood pressure were monitored. It took two months from initially using the tilt table before I was finally able to be lifted to a ninety degree angle, in February. Mum, Dad and Emma were present. It was such a momentous occasion that everyone was in tears.

Chapter 5

Rehab

After three and a half months of being in an acute hospital, I moved to a specialised rehabilitation hospital. This was a particularly bad time for me, and by the time I left I was desperate to come home.

Although I had come from a stroke ward, it had been decided that the neuro ward was more appropriate moving forward; my symptoms were more akin to those of a severe brain injury than of a classic stroke. On first impressions, I felt that the ward's decor was quite old-fashioned and it generally seemed tired in its state of repair. The sister proudly showed Emma and me around the various spaces that made up the unit, including the dining room, TV area, the large garden and gym. Being wheeled around, I noticed that the patients had a vast range of disabilities, with some not seeming to have any physical disabilities whatsoever. Glancing into the side rooms, I saw several very poorly patients who were in a comatose state and still relied on breathing apparatus. A couple had had a part of their brain and skull removed following their injuries. The ward was quite noisy with some patients shouting out in confusion.

Finally, I was shown to my bay; similar to the acute hospital, it was four-bedded but felt much less clinical in comparison. The nurse encouraged me to make my room 'homely'. I could bring a TV in or a radio if I wanted. Emma began to get my things unpacked whilst the carers hoisted me onto the bed. I was immediately greeted in bellowing tones by another patient, in his mid-fifties. He was perched on the edge of the bed next to mine, his eyes fixed on his rather loud TV. It quickly transpired that he was a very likeable character, who was always joking with the nurses. Sadly, he had an aggressive form of MS and although I didn't know it then, I would watch him rapidly deteriorate over the next few months. The patient in the bed opposite me seemed quite 'normal', capably walking around and chatting with the nurses, but when his family visited later, it became clear from their conversation that he had suffered amnesia.

My progress seemed to be slowing down, and physically I was still very much locked in. Over the next few days, I began to feel intensely aware of the reality and perhaps permanence of my condition, which triggered acute unhappiness. My thoughts spiralled to a depth of hopelessness that I had never reached before; I felt panicked and frightened. These feelings were compounded when, after just a few days, I was 'welcomed' to the rehab ward by the head of therapies, who wanted to ensure I was considering where I would go in sixty days after my stay there. She suggested perhaps a care home with some rehabilitation services. This was the first time a care home had been mentioned, and just hearing it made me feel sick to the stomach. I think Emma realised my shock and tried to wind up the conversation as quickly as possible.

One of the primary difficulties I had on this ward was due to it being largely staffed by agency workers or students who didn't know me and hadn't had any training on brain injury. Once a student nurse told me why it was good to clean teeth. As it happened, I found the experience quite amusing, but it was a poorly informed piece of advice which could have had the potential to cause a huge amount of hurt. Similarly, one of the agency carers insisted on telling me about the anatomy and function of the soft palate. If I had tried to communicate that his educational insight on the subject wasn't really necessary, it would have been me who would have appeared to be unfriendly or uninterested. As a qualified dentist, I didn't expect that a carer could add anything to my knowledge of the oral cavity, but I had to sit there and look appreciative. It is clearly sensible that everyone working on the ward would be aware of the patient's professional or special interests.

Another time, I felt an agency staff member ridiculed me. I complained to the head of ward, who assured me he would be asked to work on a different part of the ward. He came to work on the ward a number of times after this, every time on my section. Again, an agency staff gave me a jacket potato without butter, which was impossible for me to swallow. I tried to say I needed it to be moister, but she took it away before forcing me to drink normal, thin fluid (literally forcing my lips apart and pouring it in). I tried to buzz for help but my buzzer was turned off and the carer threatened to move it out of my reach. When she had gone, I buzzed because I still hadn't eaten. My buzzer was ignored for over half an hour, until a relative of a person next to me personally went to get me help. All was explained and an official complaint and incident report made, but no action was taken and the same agency carer turned up to work the next day.

My frustration as a result of miscommunication continued, but it seemed to get worse. The night staff wouldn't learn my communication despite instructions being above my bed, and it being the subject of numerous handovers. This made me especially vulnerable at night and led to more 'misunderstandings', some of which seemed a bit more deliberate than others. One night my chair was by someone else's bed and the nurse moved my supports (attachments which kept me secure in my chair) into the room where the chairs were normally kept.

Not wanting my chair to be separated from my supports, I said, 'That's my chair.'

The nurse replied, 'I am waiting for someone; I will get you ready for bed then.' Frustrated, I said, 'No. That's my chair.'

She replied, 'Do you expect me to get you ready myself?'

Exasperated, I said, 'That's my chair.'

She was very annoyed and put everyone else to bed first, leaving me to wait about an hour. Another night, at around 11:15 p.m., I asked for my neighbour's TV to be turned off; he was minimally conscious and the TV had been left by the family with the intention that the nurses turn it off before bed. The carer said, 'He says he's still watching it.' If he had said anything, it would have been a miracle. I complained again to a nurse who agreed it was too late and told the carer to turn it off. The carer began changing my neighbour and getting him ready for bed, only turning off the TV when she had finished, at about 11:45.

Sadly, these misunderstandings were not restricted to the night team. For example, I was once placed in front of my TV. Nurses would put CBeebies on and then

wonder what was wrong with me. They would guess –
'Do you want it off? Do you want it louder? Do you want
it closer?' – refusing to use my chart. I responded 'NO'
in an abrupt manner; this was usually interpreted that I
was being curt and unfriendly. In my emotionally labile
state, my frustrations appeared very demonstrative
and I probably came across as very ungrateful. But
because of my inability to communicate, I was never
able to fully explain what they were actually doing,
which was so frustrating.

'Are you too hot or too cold?' I wish, so much,
people had thought to ask me this. When I was staying
in hospital during the summer, carers would insist on
dressing me in jogging bottoms and I was placed in a
sun-trapped side room, which was already unbearable.
Despite this, carers still assumed I would want to be
covered by a sheet. Once a sheet is put on, there was
no way for me to remove it. Conversely, I also used
a pressure-relieving air mattress which continually
refilled with fresh air from the room. If it was cold,
covering me with more blankets did not change the
fact that the mattress below me was freezing.

On the door next to my bed was a poster showing a
man apparently in a similar state to me. He was staring
at the camera with pleading eyes and the caption was: 'I
need to know you care.' I don't know how much money
was spent on graphic design and photography for the

poster, but in my mind it was entirely wasted. Nurses and carers would walk right past it and then go on to treat me thoughtlessly. There were dozens of posters on that ward presented by the NHS with the aim of getting people to consider their behaviour or treatment choices, but I don't think many achieved anything other than just decorating the walls of the ward.

My mealtimes were generally a frustrating experience. Most mealtimes I either wouldn't get what I ordered or wouldn't be asked at all. When something arrived that I didn't order, I would be told that Emma had requested it, even though I knew that she hadn't. On a typical day, my food would be: lunch, jacket potato; dinner time, cheese and onion pie – which was mashed potato garnished with cheese and onions and with a side of mashed potato. They couldn't understand why I started refusing potato! One of my mealtimes, when I was undoubtedly tucking into mashed potato yet again, a patient who had had a head injury affecting his personality said that watching me eat was putting him off his food. Although I think he only said it because he himself was quite unwell, it worried me how many people thought the same but were far too polite to say so. Consequently, I ate in bed from then on, rather than in the dining room.

It was very important that I got as much sleep as possible, but night-time medication was often given after 11 p.m. and we would be woken at 6 a.m. for blood pressure observations and so on before the next shift arrived. Less than seven hours' sleep was not enough anyway, but with the noises and activity in the hospital, which were further exacerbated by staff speaking unnecessarily loudly, I didn't sleep very well at all. This happening night after night had a serious effect on my mood.

Sometimes, to my horror, if the carers couldn't find someone's single patient use manoeuvring sheet, they would simply come over to my cubicle and help themselves to mine out of my drawer, before using it for the other patient. One of them was diagnosed with MRSA (a hospital super bug) later that week. Things like this would cause me so much anger that basic rules weren't being adhered to; it just made me feel totally at the mercy of another individual's lack of respect for some of the most simple hygiene considerations. Another thing I felt strongly about was the integrity of a patient's records.

At least three times there were lies in my notes saying that I had been given fluids when I hadn't, retrospectively filling in my hourly notes at the end of the shift saying I was comfortable, didn't need changing, and had refused all drinks.

After ten months in hospital, I came to the conclusion that one of the most important jobs on the ward was the drinks round. It not only provided vital fluids to patients, who needed help with their drinking, but it was also the perfect opportunity for the nurses to monitor the fluid intake of everyone on the ward. However, this was often given to the youngest and least experienced agency carer they could find. Many times I would be asked if I wanted a drink, with them expecting a clear yes or no in reply. Despite my yes's and no's being fairly intelligible, after discovering I couldn't talk properly, they often assumed I wasn't fully cognitive and just walked away, looking a bit embarrassed that they had even spoken to me.

My time in rehab was, however, punctuated by some nice people and some funny times. My lead nurse on the ward was Vicky, and during the six and a half months of my stay on the ward, she was promoted from a nurse to a sister; an appointment I approved of. People would often call on Vicky if I was getting more and more frustrated at their inability to use my chart correctly. Vicky, on the other hand, was quite proficient at it and could often diffuse a situation by simply translating what I was trying to say.

I had to have a blood-thinning injection every night, many times given by Vicky. It usually hurt a bit so I always said 'ow' as a joke. One evening, Vicky was giving one of these injections to someone else and it genuinely hurt. He let out a scream and I burst out laughing, much to the annoyance of the patient. Vicky was trying to remain professional and not laugh. The patient made an angry, sarcastic comment about me because I was laughing.

Vicky, along with other staff, would make a point of popping to see me if they happened to be on the ward for any reason on their day off, which was very special to me. Some nurses would come over to my bed to have a chat if they were free. One of the agency staff, who had become really regular on the ward, used to clean my nose each night; I couldn't blow it myself. Another carer joined the staff while I was there, and I took to her straight away. She would often come to see me before she left for the end of her shift and I always felt a little bit calmer when she was around.

As in the acute hospital, I got on with the therapy staff. I had two sessions of each therapy – physio, speech and occupational – each week, and I looked forward to them. My physiotherapist was a similar age to me and it quickly became apparent that we shared the same sense of humour. He was very experienced, and other professionals spoke highly of him. At first, we just did passive stretches and continued to use the tilt table, but he quickly wanted to set new goals and thought that I would be able to use a standing frame if I wore platform splints to keep me stable. My right foot turned in quite badly and both feet had dropped, so I looked like a ballerina, only being able to stand on tiptoes. Without the splints there was worry that I could badly injure myself.

My speech and language therapist focused on my eating and drinking in sessions, trialling different textures of food before they could be introduced into my diet. My speech was still very unintelligible and I remained dependent on my blink chart; however, it was clearer if I could mitigate nasal escape of air, caused by paralysis of my soft palate, by wearing a nose clip, usually used for swimming. In therapy sessions, I would be hooked up to an oxygen monitor to assess how long the nose clip could be worn without it affecting my saturation levels. The speech and language therapist referred me to a maxillofacial surgeon to see whether a plate could be worn to close off my palate. I learned this could be achieved; however, wearing it would stop what little movement I had in my palate altogether, preventing it from making any recovery. I decided against the plate, and gradually I did see improvement in how intelligible my speech was without wearing the nose clip.

In conclusion, I assume my poor treatment was ordinarily carried out by people who otherwise cared. I was particularly dismayed by the covering up of genuine mistakes; it seemed the consequences for making a mistake were considered worse than potentially being caught trying to cover up. I am thinking specifically about my fluid intake chart, in which there were lies a number of times. On one occasion, Emma challenged the carer whose signature falsely confirmed I had been given a drink and her response was to just cross out her signature. When I tried to get it sorted with one of the doctors on the ward round, I was literally laughed at. I think he assumed I was too stupid to really know how many drinks I'd had.

When I was a dentist, from time to time we did make mistakes and had to admit them to the patient, and thankfully I was never questioned by the General Dental Council. However, I understood that while making a genuine mistake was forgivable, any attempt to premeditatedly try to cover up such mistakes would be met with very severe consequences.

With this in mind, if carers are too busy to fulfil their routine duties because of unforeseen circumstances, then it is important they adopt a 'no blame culture' where they can honestly explain why the mistake has been made, without fear of discipline. Without such, there is more of a temptation to try to cover up any shortcoming, which potentially presents greater danger to the patient, of which I had firsthand experience.

My nurses and carers were very busy, but in their rushing they used to make more work for themselves. I can think of a few examples of how rushing meant that far greater time was inevitably spent remedially. Firstly, no one would check my convene (a device which allowed me to go to the toilet without having to specifically move) before they hoisted me into my chair, which would take about thirty seconds. So I used to wet myself and it would take two people forty minutes to change me. Secondly, the person on the drinks round would not have time to give me my drink so they would leave it by my bed for someone else to give me. It would go cold and be taken away. In the end I wouldn't get enough fluids, suffering three urine infections, which required a nurse having to give me a five-minute infusion of antibiotics three times a day. Lastly, at night about three staff would spend half an hour trying to work out what I wanted. This happened most nights during my first few months, but no one would find ten minutes to learn my communication chart.

Having spent nearly a year in hospital, people might think I have a fantastic insight into what's wrong with NHS hospitals and have a few suggestions as to how they could be improved. Believe it or not, I am still baffled as to why the care seems so uncompassionate. I can certainly confirm all the 'horror' stories told. But whereas you might expect me to say these were mainly perpetrated by people who were only carers in order to earn money, although these people existed, much of my poor treatment was actually carried out by 'caring carers'. So what was it that made these caring individuals act so insensitively?

In my mind, there were too many rules and regulations hampering good carers who would otherwise use a bit of common sense and do the right thing anyway. Much of the bureaucracy was put in place to ensure a really poor, unthinking carer was limited as to the harm they could inflict if they just followed a set of rules, but for the vast majority these rules seemed to form a 'straightjacket' that disabled them from doing their job in the best way they saw fit. I don't know whether this is one of the reasons for the lack of compassion described in a report in 2012 (see http://www.dailymail. co.uk/health/article-2084534/Damning-report-finds-NHS-staff-lack-ability-compassion-job.html), but it was certainly an observation I made time after time.

Chapter 6

Coming Home

I had spent three and a half months in the acute hospital and was coming to the end of my allotted sixty days in rehab. I was unsure as to where I would end up next. The only two prospects that I thought I had at that time were to go to a private rehabilitation centre, or into a nursing home. I couldn't see how returning home would work. How would Emma cope? Even if she did have assistance with carers coming in an hour here and an hour there, I needed twenty-four hour care. I couldn't put this on Emma; besides, most things needed two people. My main concern was who would deal with me going to the toilet. I could never allow our relationship to overstep that mark.

I had been coming home for visits every week since Emma's birthday in March 2012. Our home was completed just three weeks before I returned for that first visit. Was it just incredible fortune that our home had been undergoing an extension when I got unwell? In January 2011, just ten months before my stroke, we began planning the extension and alteration to the internal layout of our house. We arranged to make it more open plan so it felt airy. We proposed patio doors, which would open right up and provide an equal level between the kitchen floor and the patio. Finally, having given Emma her bath upstairs during the previous summer, I wanted a wet room at the back of the house for me. I had owned two different homes over the past seven years but neither was in any way accessible. By chance, two months before my life changed forever, we began a six-month build that would make our home in Bournville perfectly appropriate for a disabled person. However, the accessibility of our home was useless without the right care support.

If there was no way of me going home, a nursing home would literally be my worst nightmare. I was terrified of this prospect. I knew the system; if I went in, I was sure I would never come out. So the private rehabilitation unit it had to be. Emma and I began setting our sights on this centre as our one and only option. Emma, her mum and my friend Dan had already visited earlier on in the year and reported back that it was at least modern and clean and there were other people of similar age to me, who had also suffered brain injuries. I could stay here for six months or so;

perhaps then I would be more independent and could reconsider coming home. Emma petitioned to get the professionals on our side: my consultant seemed supportive and the Continuing Health Care (CHC) nurse agreed to fight our corner with the commissioners. Emma also rallied people to pray for the funding to be approved. It simply had to work out.

However, in May 2012, to my terror, the funding was declined for me to go to this unit; it was simply too expensive. Instead, I had to live out my nightmare where I was, and was granted another sixty days. I was devastated, panicked, terrified. It was inconceivable that I had to stay here in a place where I felt so very vulnerable. Emma was devastated too. She had fought so hard to get me the outcome I wanted. It felt like we were back to square one. I was inconsolable for the rest of the day, letting out bellows of sobs until I was so exhausted that it felt like there were no tears left for me to shed. Emma sat close by, attempting to console me. It was around this time that Emma had a conversation with my physiotherapist, who said that I had the right to have the help that I needed at home if I so wished; perhaps live-in carers? Later, Emma broached the subject with me. It was certainly an option and I began to see a small shaft of hope for my future. I still had reservations. Who would these live-in carers be? How would we cope with having strangers living in our home?

Emma began conversations with our CHC nurse, and by the beginning of July, the prospect of coming home was becoming more real. She suggested a specialised live-in care agency, who supported others with complex conditions like my own. Carers would rotate, perhaps doing two weeks on and two weeks off with Emma remaining on hand to assist. Emma being there helped me feel at ease but it niggled me to think about what would happen when Emma went out. How would they understand me? Still, anything was better than being in hospital. I had a goal in sight to get home as soon as possible. Once my second allocation of sixty days was up and the funding was finally agreed for the correct care package, the medical team began arranging for my discharge, which I was told would be the 17 August. From then on, I began counting the days. My occupational therapist ordered my equipment: a hoist, a profiling hospital bed, a standing frame, slings, slide sheets... She also arranged to have a training session for Emma and my parents so they knew exactly how to hoist me safely. All things seemed to be in place. I continued to feel just as vulnerable on the ward but my panic was mitigated by knowing there was an end in sight.

On 14 August, just three days before my agreed discharge, I received news that the personal assistant (PA) the care agency had timetabled was ill and so my discharge date would have to be moved back. A cyclone of fear hit me and I felt completely powerless. Having spent ten months in hospital, I just simply couldn't face another moment of being so intensely vulnerable, not having my basic needs met, but how could I blame the care agency for an employee falling ill? The only power I felt I had was to refuse food. Maybe that would get people to take things seriously. I had threatened this before but this time it seemed like my only option and so the hunger strike began. I was going home that day for a visit, so I announced my intention to Emma, who seemed to accept it calmly but disappeared to ring her dad. I remained in the kitchen, staring out at our garden, which was covered by a dense, black cloud, pouring rain. I remembered a story in the Bible about a rainbow signalling hope and wondered where my rainbow was. Over the next five minutes, whilst staring out blankly, the clouds parted, a rainbow formed and minutes later there were blue skies. I was shocked. I didn't believe for one minute God would do anything so simplistic to show me I had hope, but I had just witnessed something immediately after praying for it. I couldn't imagine it was God, but the thought that it could be caused me to prematurely end my hunger strike and, to Emma's relief, I tucked into lunch.

During my illness many people had supported us financially through collections, sponsored events and personal generosity, but many more wanted to help financially, not knowing how. Formerly, I had been involved with supporting a charity who sought to end all types of human trafficking. One Sunday, when I was attending church from hospital, we had a special presentation by the charity Hope for Justice, and Pastor Stuart announced a plan to walk the length of Birmingham to raise awareness and money. I lay awake most of that night recalling some of the harrowing stories we had heard. I was a prisoner too, but I was surrounded by people who loved me, whereas many of these slaves were isolated and alone in their suffering. I decided to do the walk myself and to add an additional challenge, pledged to do it in a normal wheelchair without a headrest. Many of my friends and former colleagues were just waiting for an opportunity to support me and my sponsorship was both generous and overwhelming. I was able to raise £4,500, contributing to nearly half of our church's overall support of about £10,000. Following the success of the walk, I was unwilling to give up my more normal-shaped wheelchair and return to my big tilting one.

Eventually, on 2 September 2012, I finally came home and straight away had a party to celebrate. When we got talking to our PA, we learned he had spent the previous week with another client, which had been scheduled at the last minute. He was told that the change of plan was because my house wasn't ready for me to come home. I was furious! We had finished all alterations to the house six months earlier and it seemed the care agency had too many clients and not enough PAs and we realised this new provider of services was no better than the rehab centre in regards to their approach to integrity.

Coming home was like a holiday in comparison to my time of being in rehab. We had set up a hospital bed in our former dining room and my granddad's old recliner in our extension. For the first few days Emma slept on a mattress on the floor next to my bed and, to my amazement, slept lightly enough for me to get her attention with my voice. Formerly, she could only be woken with dynamite! For the first time in over ten months, I could look forward to mealtimes and enjoy a night's sleep without additional noises. Being unable to talk meant that I was acutely lonely in hospital yet now I had company twenty-four hours a day.

I kept the carers I was given for four months. They were both Eastern European and although they could speak English very well, they couldn't understand me so they seemed to only be Emma's auxiliaries as any communication between them and I would have to go via Emma. During this time we learned a lot about how my care needed to be improved.

In the first week at home, I was having a shower in

my new shower chair but wasn't tilted back enough, so when I sneezed, my weight shot forward and I came right out of the chair and landed with a thud on the shower room floor. Thankfully my fall was broken by striking my head on a hollow wood panel door, which was fairly soft in comparison to the hard slate floor. I really frightened myself and bruised my leg, but otherwise I was unscathed. My PA, on the other hand, who witnessed the fall, unable to respond quickly enough, gave himself such a fright that he couldn't eat for the rest of the day. A lesson learned early on was to tilt back the shower chair far enough and to always have two people to shower me. This time, thankfully, there were no serious consequences.

A few weeks later, I was sitting on my standing frame, waiting to be secured and elevated to a standing position. My PA pulled on my legs and I felt my weight shift to the side. Unable to correct myself or mitigate my fall in any way, my body collapsed onto the slate kitchen floor with my head landing first. Lying dazed, my body still crumpled up, a shocked Emma and my PA began to unfold my limp limbs, which were twisted at awkward angles under my body. We called an ambulance and they chose to use a full spinal board and blocks to immobilise my body, while they transported me to hospital. I underwent various tests and CT scans to establish if I had done any damage. I didn't have much faith in that A&E department as a year before I had walked in there and never walked again! I was terrified about what further damage had been done by my fall; up until now I had been trying to stay positive after the initial stroke. However, I didn't want to live anymore if I was going to have any further disability, which I made clear to Emma. When I returned home, I remained dizzy for a few days but the doctor assured me this was concussion as opposed to anything more sinister. Another lesson learned: always have one person holding me while the other person secured me when putting me in my standing frame.

Just before Christmas, a further two months later, I was still sleeping downstairs. One morning I was getting ready and my arm fell against the hot radiator. At first I just said 'ARM' to the carer to alert her, but she just looked at me with not even a flicker of recognition about what I was saying. As it continued to burn through the layers of my skin, I became more and more distressed whilst my speech became even less intelligible. Seeing my distress, she fetched my blink chart. As my arm continued melting and I was unable to remove it, I became increasingly panicked. Realising my panic, my carer became flustered herself and couldn't use my chart. In the end, I screamed for Emma, who was having a shower. Emma came and moved my arm and we realised we couldn't tolerate carers who couldn't communicate. At a meeting attended by our care coordinator and CHC nurse, we requested only British PAs. It was explained this would be difficult as 90 per cent of employees were Eastern European, but because weeks had passed, and I was still sporting the scar on my elbow, my CHC nurse insisted the care agency acted upon my request. We began to receive more appropriate PAs, who we could relate to more like friends. These continued to change every few months, as being a live-in PA is not really a long-term career choice.

When I left the rehab centre I was placed on a waiting list for additional therapy to continue for sixteen weeks once I was home. This didn't start for another six weeks and it seemed many sessions were used up in goal-planning meetings, midway review meetings and final discharge meetings. I hated those meetings; they were always so negative, pessimistic about my prognosis, and I always felt pressured into accepting their suggestions for the future. When this therapy finished in January 2013, Emma fought to maintain a small amount of NHS physiotherapy every few weeks. But just months later this finished too, and I just couldn't face any more arguments or planning meetings. When I was a student, I learned about the inverse care law that corresponded to dental provision; it said: 'Those most in need of care are those least likely to receive it.' I couldn't believe

I had become a victim. So we were forced to give up on NHS therapy altogether and concentrated our time and resources seeking private help. We had been paying for our own private hydrotherapy and now also sought land physiotherapy through the private sector. Our blessings became very stark to Emma and I; we were able to afford to commission my own therapy and do away with a huge slice of NHS bureaucracy overnight. Because I was implicitly made to feel like I was wasting resources by the NHS teams, I felt that a burden had been lifted. We were haunted, however, by the knowledge that many other people who could not afford private physiotherapy would be left as they were until they died, and the additional realization that that could have been me.

When I came out of hospital I had been tormented by memories and injustices I had experienced and, unable to break free from them, I wrote them down as a therapeutic exercise to try to lay them to rest when I first came home. During the initial months, all my energy was ploughed into just getting better so I tried not to think of any implications of treatment given in the lead-up to the stroke. However, as the months progressed, I became increasingly angry when I thought of it. Eighteen months had passed and I was still battling with unresolved emotions, perhaps because the GP and osteopath were still oblivious to the condition that I had been left with. I was angry at the GP. I felt that if she had told me prayer works for her and recommended a church I could visit to get help, she would have probably lost her job, but instead she endorsed a private osteopath and nearly sent me to my death. I was also angry at the osteopath himself. Although I recognise he didn't cause the initial headaches, I am sure his manipulation at least made things much worse or may have even caused the stroke, with it being immediately after the manipulation that I began experiencing symptoms. Needing some sort of closure, I decided to write to both professionals reminding them of their dealings with me and informing them of the predicament that I now faced. I also requested my notes. The notes from the GP reflected exactly my recollection of the appointment, and although in hindsight I do not believe it was appropriate to send me to a private osteopath, it made me feel like it was genuinely done in good faith. In contrast to the GP, what the osteopath provided did not reflect whatsoever my memory of our meeting. I don't know whether his notes were rewritten in response to my request or whether they were done defensively at the time, realising the gravity of his actions.

Chapter 7

Church

When I was growing up, I was part of a fairly traditional Methodist church in rural Burscough, Lancashire. They had an old-fashioned pipe organ and sang hymns. It was quite a modernisation when our church first got an electronic organ, which still sounded like the old pipe organ. Going to church was out of compulsion when I was young, and having grown up with friends at church, when I was a teenager, I obviously wanted to spend time with my friends and I thought at the time that was all church was.

I started university in Birmingham in 1997, which was seen by many of my family as an answer to prayer. At the end of my first year A-levels, I only got a D in chemistry, which was a far cry from the B I needed to study dentistry. So the following year my mum and dad paid for a private tutor and my family spent many hours in prayer. I, however, felt it was just my hard work and self-effort and that there was nothing divine about it. The fact that my parents and grandparents had prayed for me just seemed a coincidence. After all, there were plenty of my colleagues who had got into dental school based on hard work and not prayer.

Having started university, I didn't find a church straight away and quickly stopped looking as having a lie-in on a Sunday morning after the night before became more important. There didn't seem to be any immediate downsides to missing church, but as time went on I began to realise whatever enjoyment I might experience during the week would always seem to have an attached unpleasant side-effect; for example, going out drinking was a favourite pastime but always seemed to be coupled with an unpleasant hangover.

After three years, I began to really feel the effects of the absence of a church community. I began to attend the C of E church opposite my house. It was quite an older congregation and so they were really excited to have 'new blood' and made me feel really welcome. Being back in a church family felt comforting. Choosing to go to church caused me to have more questions about what a Christian belief was really about, so after two years, when I'd finally finished my five-year degree, and the vicar left for a new post up north, I started attending an Alpha course at Christian Life Centre in Selly Oak. I thought the church services were a bit mad, and not my cup of tea at all! They were clapping, and genuinely singing as opposed to the reverent mumbling I was used to. However, the people at the Alpha course seemed OK, and after a few weeks, during which I had learned an incredible amount about myself and the God who I claimed to follow, I started to attend the Sunday morning worship. I cannot claim to have had a 'light bulb' epiphany during Alpha, but in hindsight it was certainly the catalyst for my life changing completely.

During the first few weeks after I became unwell, there were thousands of people praying, and I know many other churches followed my progress. We used to get cards and letters from churches we had never heard of saying that they were regularly praying for my situation; there were even churches on other continents who were aware of me, and praying for me. In the first few days after my stroke, many of our church family were ringing Emma for an update, and having to repeatedly explain the direness of the situation became overwhelming for her. So to try to keep everyone informed, our church set up a blog that could be updated by the church office or by Emma herself. The blog has been updated ever since and as I write this it has had 65,000 views worldwide.

There were three churches in particular that consistently supported me and my family. My mum and dad's church, Burscough Methodist, was where I grew up and attended Scouts and took part in the annual pantomime. The church's love for God, demonstrated by their sense of community and pastoral care, gave me assurance that Mum and Dad would have all the prayer and practical support they needed. The church community later did some fundraising for me by organising a sponsored bike ride along the cycle paths and canals from the church in Burscough to my home now, in Bournville – about 200 miles. They raised an incredible £12,000 for a specialist active/passive bike. They are normally the reserve of a rehabilitation gym, but now I had my own. The remaining money I put towards my tuition fees for university, studying theology. Of course, the money raised was valuable practically, but knowing that many people I had grown up with still cared, even though I had not seen many of them for years, had even greater emotional value.

Then there was the church Emma used to attend, Renewal, where her father was still an elder. Emma had grown up in the church and was best friends with the daughter of David, the senior pastor. Pastor David had become a little like a second dad to Emma, and when we started dating I needed to undergo his own interrogation for approval too.

Then, of course, there was our church, Christian Life Centre. Having completed the Alpha course in 2002, I was later baptised there. I started helping with the youth work and later began hosting a home group for young adults. When Emma and I met, we knew we were going to have to choose a church; I felt it was right to stay at CLC, but not wanting to influence Emma's decision in any way, I kept quiet about my feelings. A few weeks later, Emma decided it would be nice to support me at CLC and perhaps discover a new challenge, away from the shadow of her youth. Within weeks of being married, Emma and I were serving together at CLC.

A week after my stroke, our church arranged a prayer meeting specifically to pray for me. It was attended by nearly 300 people, and prayer meetings followed on a Thursday in Burscough and Friday at CLC. The prayer meeting on Friday became especially important for Emma. She was given much support individually, and often came away uplifted and able to encourage me. There were dozens of people who chose to specifically pray for our situation continuously. Once when we were at a conference at the NEC, we met a man who we had never seen before and he told us he set his alarm every evening at 7 p.m. so that he could pray daily for Emma and me.

Many of the things our church did to support me and my family I never knew about at the time. When I was in the ITU I could only have one visitor at a time. Therefore, many of my family were spending hours in the waiting room whilst taking it in turns to see me. The church ensured there was always a pastor or elder looking after my family in the waiting room. In addition, many meals were provided for Mum, Dad, Emma and whoever was visiting me.

Gandhi once said, 'I like your Christ, I do not like your Christians. Your Christians are so unlike your Christ.' I was discovering the opposite, that God's church was keeping me and my family in their hearts, but any input from God Himself seemed conspicuous in its absence. I read an excellent book called *God on Mute* by Pete Greig (Kingsway, 2007), which suggested all the nice things others do are a gift from God to you; in which case God was far from being absent, He was surely showering me with gifts, but I could not feel it.

Joan is a lady from church with whom I have a close friendship. When I first had the stroke, I was unable to see visitors, but Joan decided to get the bus to the hospital and sit in the corridor outside my ward and pray; she was only yards away from me, but I never knew. When I was a bachelor, she used to help me by doing some cleaning and ironing and our friendship developed to the point where we looked after each other. We used to joke about Joan being like a second mum to me! On our wedding day, Joan was invited, of course. Having never met my brother-in-law, when she was asked which side of the family she knew, she proudly said, 'What do you mean? I'm the mother of the groom.' My brother-in-law hadn't met my mother either, but Joan is an Afro-Caribbean lady and it was clear she couldn't be my mother; still, she answered the question so seriously, it caused a lot of nervous laughter.

My first Christmas was spent in hospital. In the morning, Emma and her mum and dad took me to the hospital chapel. One of the ways my stroke has affected me is that I have very high emotional lability. This means my emotions, like crying, frustration or laughter, are very close to the surface. When everyone started to sing I was unable to control my laughter, which at the time was particularly loud; my laughing set Emma and her mum off and we had to leave early! A number of friends took time to visit me on Christmas Day, including the associate pastor, Emanuel, and all his family; my friend Pastor Stuart and his two sons also came to visit.

When I had the stroke, we had just begun our extension, and although we had professional architects who were friends from the church, Pearl and Michael, to draw up plans, I was project managing the job myself. On hearing of my stroke, Pearl and Michael immediately took over the project management, and when I was a bit better, Michael used to come into hospital to see me to get my opinion on certain ideas or materials. We ended up with our extension professionally project managed for us.

I had a number of insurance policies in case something like this happened to me, but most were still in my name because I never expected to be completely incapacitated. Another friend from church, who was also a lawyer, was able to gain my consent with a series of blinks to give Emma power of attorney so she could access my accounts.

As I mentioned earlier, when I was at the acute hospital I made it to church on Christmas Day, and once more when Stuart, my senior pastor, arranged a service for a number of my friends to come in to the hospital chapel, so I could be included. Normally, however, my church was a chaplain coming once a week and reading a scripture and praying for me.

When I went into rehab, I started attending hospital chapel on a Sunday. On some Tuesdays, I also went to Emma's old church, where they had a healing service. I explained to Stuart that I could cope with the relative anonymity of it there, but I wasn't ready to return to our church. After six months, two friends were getting married and invited Emma and I, but the ceremony was going to be at CLC; it would be my first time back there since my stroke. As I approached the doors, I could feel my heart pounding in my chest and was feeling really sick. I took my place and then, looking around, the feelings of betrayal by God became too much and I broke down. After all I had done for God, how could He leave me like this? I suppose it was then that I realised my service to God and the church was not supposed to be work that afforded me special treatment, and it made me really consider what my motives had always been. After this, visits to CLC became more regular.

I understand it's not easy for people to always take the time to discover a deep and meaningful faith of their own, but quite apart from faith, I cannot understand how people can deal with this sort of situation without the massive support of a church family; not just the three church communities mentioned, but the church as a global body of people.

Just under two years after my stroke I had to undergo an operation to place a pump under my skin and insert a tiny tube into my spine to deliver a drug which would alleviate my spasms. I was terrified about having the operation, but my need for the drug to relieve my spasms was so great I pushed any fears about the procedure to the back of my mind until I was literally on the trolley waiting to be operated on. When I came around from the operation I was in a lot of pain, and I remember the anaesthetist giving me some additional morphine to try to control it, and then he left me to the care of two recovery nurses. After coming round fully, I was returned to the ward where Emma was actually waiting. One nurse knew Emma and me from our church, which she also attended. We had become used to quite a number of health care professionals who treated me being Christians; however, this seemed like a step further. It was as if God wasn't going to leave my care to just any theatre recovery nurse, although I am sure they are generally excellent anyway, but He was specifically ensuring that my care was going to be provided by someone who knew me from our church.

Now, when I attend church it feels like a therapy much the same as my physical therapy. For example, going to church and allowing others to pray for me in person were originally just an act of my will and not a result of what I felt like doing. When I was a youth leader, I used to explain that our feelings weren't always true and therefore not a reliable indicator of our situation; for example, watching a scary movie does not put us in any danger whatsoever, however, our feelings might tell us otherwise. So it's important we live by something more substantial. Three years on, my feelings have caught up with what I chose to do, and now I love going to church.

Chapter 8

Emma

When I was twenty-eight, one of my friends really wanted to go to a Christian speed-dating event and as I was single, and often grumbling about how I would never meet someone, I had very few excuses not to go along. At the event, we were assured it wasn't speed dating, but 'Christian networking'. Very few men had turned up and there were no age categories, so women were talking to each other and I was talking to fifty-five-year-olds, who assured me that they could wonderfully match-make me with their daughters!

Of course, the whole event seemed awkward. I was simply making a judgement of potential partners based on their physical appearance and five minutes of role play; the first half of the evening left me with an increasing feeling that I shouldn't have come. After a brief interval in the bar area, we returned to the function room to be told that instead of following the normal speed-dating format, we could speak to anyone; however, the same rule applied that we had to 'move on' when the bell rang. I had spotted Emma in the first half. She was beautiful, about 5 foot 7 with mid-length blonde hair. I must admit I was suspicious about why she was single. After talking to a few people, I saw Emma and made a beeline to speak to her. I learned that she was only twenty-two. I wouldn't have thought that I would go for someone that much younger than me, but she seemed fairly mature and self-assured and the conversation flowed. Emma was working as a support assistant for teenagers with learning difficulties and had also taught holiday Spanish for a local college some evenings, and wanted to pursue a career in Further Education. We chatted for our allotted five minutes. To my delight, when the bell went Emma continued talking, just carrying on as if nothing had happened and leaving me with the hope that the attraction was mutual. I spoke to one other person that night but couldn't stop thinking about the young blonde.

The friend I came with had finally had enough, and so we left before the evening came to a natural close. I was a little curious to know if my attraction was reciprocated, so on a whim I put Emma's secret identity symbol down on my paper before handing it in.

The following day I still couldn't get Emma out of

my mind. It happened to be the Saturday that I was scheduled to see emergency patients at the Walsall Walk In Centre. I checked my phone between patients, but no text came. Driving home, I heard the text message alert but being on the fast lane of the motorway, there was no way I could respond. I panicked. If I left it too long, she might think I wasn't interested. As soon as I got a chance to pull over, I did. Emma had been given my details and wanted to know if I wanted to catch up. That weekend we exchanged texts and arranged to meet on the Monday evening for dinner. Emma lived in Solihull, a town about eight miles from where I lived in south Birmingham. She suggested that we go to one of the bars in the town centre that served good food. She looked stunning. Emma chose a salad and I, not being so concerned about how it looked, ordered the biggest burger on the menu! I remember watching Emma trying to eat her salad; she was shaking so much that by the time her fork met her mouth everything had fallen off. It was quite endearing. We talked about holidays, our churches, work, friends. Conversation was easy. We also learned that we knew some of the same people; I was volunteering alongside one of Emma's close friends with Teen Challenge. At the end of the night, I asked if I could see Emma again and she thankfully agreed.

And so our relationship progressed. To begin with,

we kept in touch by text and met about once a week. I was keen to impress and made every effort to wine and dine, so to speak. Emma met my parents about six weeks into our relationship and, although it was clear Emma and I were completely different, they seemed to see we fitted together perfectly. After only three months of dating, it was clear to me that Emma was 'the one' and from then on we began talking about our future together. It was definitely a whirlwind romance. By November, I had decided to propose, so I arranged a visit with David, Emma's dad, on a day when I was certain Emma would be at college. I expected it was a father's privilege to make a future son-in-law sweat, but there was no such torture. He told me how proud he was of Emma before saying how he would be happy for me to propose, so I left with all sorts of ideas whizzing round my head about how I could make it memorable. The next day, we had already planned to go to Broadway, a small touristy village in the Cotswolds. During lunch, the conversation drifted onto marriage and Emma asked me if I were to propose around Christmas, when did I think would be an appropriate time of year to get married? I thought about it casually and suggested perhaps the summer would be sensible. At this point Emma took out her diary and started asking about more specific dates. I was taken aback by her forwardness, but we continued the day without anything else said about it. On the Sunday, we were going to Emma's church. I pulled up outside the house and Emma got in. As she did, she said excitedly, as though the words were tumbling uncontrollably out of her mouth: 'We're going to get married soon!'

I flashed a quick glance across. 'You know something!' Emma crumpled under even this simple interrogation, and the story emerged. Emma had finished college early the day I had been to see her father, and arrived home to find my car on the driveway. Guessing my reasons for being there, she continued around onto the next cul-de-sac before ringing some of her best friends and announcing our imminent engagement! She then went home and interrogated her father, who buckled in no time, being unable to lie.

Although, the element of surprise was diminished, I still had the opportunity of the ring. Instead of choosing it between us, I was going to pick the ring myself and present it to Emma as a surprise, so one night I contacted her sister through Facebook and asked for her help in choosing a favourable style. My betrayal was almost immediate as she contacted Emma to find out what she should suggest. On the Thursday I went to choose a ring, and later all Emma wanted to know was if I had been shopping. That night she was teaching and apologised to her Spanish class for being so excited, announcing it was only because her boyfriend had been out to buy an engagement ring for her that very day. I decided to surprise her in what little way I could; she wouldn't expect me to be waiting for her at home. I parked my car around the corner and waited in the living room. As Emma came in her parents walked out. Seeing me, Emma was both shocked and excited as she anticipated the question, which was the subject of the most poorly kept secret. She saw the bag in my hand, took it and ran to the sofa to open it.

We were married in the following July before Emma moved into my blokey bachelor pad in Harborne; however, Emma insisted on emasculating our new bedroom. We had been told by quite a few newly-weds to expect the first year of marriage to be the hardest; if we could just survive that, it would get much easier. Conversely, Emma and I found our first year of marriage to be wonderful. Just after our first anniversary, we moved to a new house we had chosen between us in Bournville. We had really stretched ourselves financially, but neither of us could have imagined just two and a half years later my life insurance would pay for the house in full for us.

We continued to live what seemed like the perfect marriage, never arguing and playing to each other's strengths. I was fiercely logical and pragmatic, whereas Emma was far more emotional and able to demonstrate empathy. Between us we led the young adults group at

Our Wedding Day in 2008

Emma and I enjoying a cruise

Paul and I climbing together

Emma and I enjoying our skiing holiday

Snow and ice climbing
after staying overnight in a shelter.

Climbing Tryfan North Ridge –
one of my favourite scrambles.

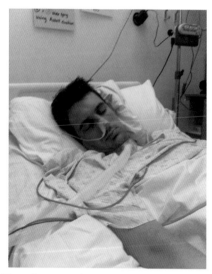

First few weeks in an induced coma

My first time outside

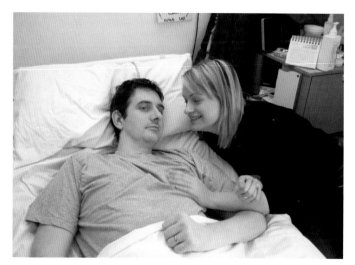

Emma and I

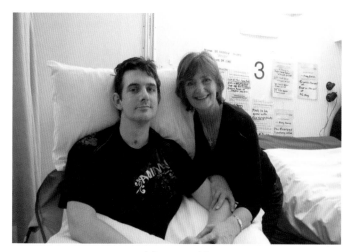

Mum and I

Harry's Wedding

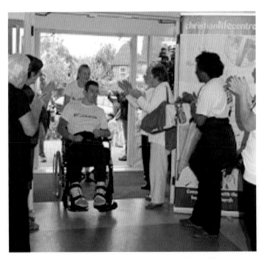

Finishing my sponsored walk

Best-man for my brother Paul and sister-in-law Katie.

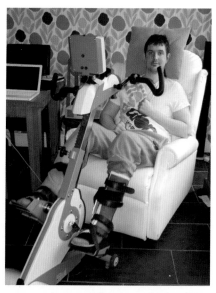

On my cycle machine bought by friends
from Burscough Methodist Church

Emma and I enjoying life

Meeting Onesimus the dog who loves me as I am.

church and enjoyed socialising in our new home. Of course, like any couple, we did have some challenges. Emma had struggled with times of depression and anxiety since she was a teenager, and during our marriage there were some incidents of this becoming more acute. It didn't really faze me, because when we recited our marriage vows, I was fully aware of the possible consequences of making those promises – what they might mean in terms of the support that I might need to give – but I never imagined that Emma's promises to me would be tested so severely.

***

It was clear from the moment of my stroke that Emma wasn't going to make my care the sole responsibility of the professionals and, as well as learning how to suction my tracheostomy, she was aggressively defending my interests amongst the many high-ranking doctors looking after me. I remember one of the first things Emma did was insist they put my full name and title, Dr Andrew Davies, above my bed, and not just my nickname, so that people wouldn't talk down to me. When I got unwell, my parents moved down to Birmingham to live in our house with Emma. I was aware Emma was very different to my parents, and was unsure what it would be like under such pressure. Although my mum and dad had always got along with Emma very well, it was a new test for their relationship. Within days, it became obvious to them why I had fallen in love with Emma, and Mum and Dad really accepted her as a second daughter.

On the ward, if the other patients had guests who came outside visiting times, they would be asked politely but firmly to come back during visiting hours. Emma, however, had become like one of the members of staff, being allowed to use the fridge and microwave in the ward's staff room and come to be with me anytime, whether it was visiting times or not. She was the only person who could effectively communicate with me, so it was in everyone's interests to let Emma stay. It was quite early on that I was able to communicate to Emma that I was getting panic attacks and that I needed something to help relieve my spasms.

After Christmas, my catheter was removed and I had to literally toilet train again. Although I didn't have much control over my bladder, I knew a few seconds before I needed a wee. It was just long enough to close the curtains and place a urine bottle in time for me to go to the toilet. On one occasion, during the rush of closing curtains and placing the urine bottle, I suffered some trauma and was unable to tell Emma she was hurting me. Next morning when I was being washed by the carer, she noticed some blood and immediately got the doctor to establish what was wrong. I was trying to communicate that it was OK, it had been done by Emma. The doctor assured me it was normal to want to carry on marital relationships in hospital, but we needed to be more careful. I was mortified. I tried frantically to explain she had got it wrong, but I was unable to make her understand. That morning my mum and dad came to visit and the moment my mum arrived I spelt out: 'TELL THE DR EMMA TRAUMATISED ME WITH WEE BOTTLE.' It was one of the times when Mum understood exactly which letters I was selecting – she wrote them all down in her prayer journal – but they spelt a sentence that didn't make any sense at all!

Emma visited nearly every day for ten months while I was in hospital, and if she was ever away with work she would ensure Mum and Dad were in Birmingham and available to sit with me in her absence. Emma's care continued at the rehab centre, where she would often come in before visiting, to give me my food. I remember one occasion my food arrived and it was a vegetable lasagne. Anyone who knew me would have been aware this would have been very low down on my choices if I had been asked, but because asking was difficult I often got what I was given. Emma told me there was also ham and mushroom pie for tea that night, and knowing I would prefer that, she went to see if there was any left. She returned triumphantly with a plate of ham and mushroom pie, but while she was adjusting a chair in order to feed me, she let it drop on the floor right by my bed. I was desperately trying to scrape it up with my eyes and to make things worse it turned out to be the last piece, so I ended up with my vegetable lasagne after all.

When I was a dentist I used to have something I called my professional shield. This meant I was genuinely able to care for my patients and really empathise when they were frightened, but their situation or fear never affected me so much that I couldn't think as clearly as normal, or indeed operate. This professional shield never let me down for ten years, except once when I was working in the emergency centre. We had had a phone call from the local psychiatric unit; they had a patient in severe pain. We told them to send him down straight away, and they said his wife would bring him immediately. After we had taken a full history, we established he had had a complete mental breakdown and was constantly terrified; he had been nervous about dental work before so this was an unbearable situation. He was in a wheelchair with a frozen look on his face, unable to speak or move. His breakdown had clearly had a devastating effect on his appearance and life in general. His wife, on the other hand, was very smart and well-presented, almost glamorous. Her love for the man in the chair was palpable as she caressed him and attempted to calm him down, reassuring him I was both competent and not at all hesitant about what needed to be done. I had done nothing to deserve such confidence being placed on me. That day the man was treated by Andy, with tears in my eyes, and not Dr Andrew Davies, who normally took over at the beginning of a working day. I had to leave the room as soon as I had finished. I wonder whether Emma's manner has disarmed anyone else's professional shield during my treatment.

When I first came home, I made a real effort to face my insecurities and embarrassment to go out with Emma as much as I could, so that she could continue to enjoy aspects of a more normal life with her husband, such as going to restaurants and taking days out. As my spasms got worse, this became much harder. Emma is very good at not just telling me she loves me but showing it by all the things she does for me every day. I am secure enough in our relationship to know that Emma won't ever leave me, but I am haunted by the fact that Emma couldn't possibly be more eligible. She's beautiful, has a lovely home, paid for fully, and a secure financial future. She's still only twenty-nine and she could easily find someone else and have a perfect life; the only thing standing in the way of this is me. Perhaps it's best I am not legally allowed to end my own life because the perceived additional pressure to do so by society would be huge.

My disability has put our marriage under enormous

strain. Before the stroke, I remember only arguing once with Emma, whereas a combination of my frustration and difficulty communicating means that we have misunderstandings more regularly. I think, however, that people will look at our relationship and see the strength that lies behind those momentary outbursts of frustration. A technique we learned for communication during our marriage preparation course was only used during this one argument prior to my stroke. However, since my communication has been compromised, it has proved itself invaluable. This technique is, in essence, that I say what is bothering me and before Emma is allowed to respond, she must repeat back, in her own words, what she interpreted. Only when I have confirmed that she was hearing correctly, is she allowed to reply back. Afterwards, I have to repeat the same process with Emma. It is a time-consuming and laborious process, but one we both find very cathartic, and it tends to resolve any misunderstandings.

A specific difficulty I have with communication is that my voice has no intonation, so rather than it sounding like a proper sentence, my voice sounds like it's simply reciting a list of imperatives without punctuation. Similar to when people misinterpret unpunctuated text messages, I find strings of key words can have very different meanings without intonation. My tone, especially when I am frustrated, can also come across as aggressive, even though this is not direct frustration with Emma, but with my disability. Of course, Emma tends to react to this if she interprets that I am unjustly directing my frustration at her; this can escalate into an argument. Following lots of discussion, Emma is improving on not hearing an aggressive intent in my frustration, and we are having much fewer misunderstandings than when I first came out of hospital.

Chapter 9

Family

Within hours of the initial onset of my stroke, my mum, dad and brother, Paul, had travelled the two-hour journey to be with me. I say 'my stroke'; at that time, I hadn't realised that I had had a stroke, but on hearing what my symptoms were, Mum and Dad must have been worried. Tina, my sister, followed as soon as she could organise my nephews, three-year-old Luke and four-month-old Jake. I remember Emma telling me all the family were on their way but, in my confused state, I wondered why they were being so dramatic. Paul, Mum and Dad had made it in time when my right-hand side and voice were still working, but later that night the stroke worsened and I became locked in.

About a week later, when I came round from my sedation, I was aware that Mum and Dad were effectively living in Birmingham, and Tina and Paul seemed to be there most of the time. When I was particularly ill, Paul expressed his frustration that Tina, with her mothering instincts, seemed to know just what to do and say, whereas he was struggling to do the right thing, but I just felt comforted that they were there. I was the middle of the three of us, both in age and location; Tina had made her home in London, where she met my brother-in-law, Keith, and was raising my two nephews. Paul had remained close to where we grew up in West Lancashire, and he was working for the police there, so living in Birmingham I saw quite a lot of both of them.

Eight days after my stroke, when I left the ITU and moved up to the stroke ward, a speech and language therapist showed me an alphabet board and said my name began with 'A' and could I blink when she pointed to the line which contained an 'A'. She of course pointed straight to it and I blinked. She then asked me to blink when she pointed to the correct letter on that line. She asked if I knew what the second letter of my name was. I blinked once to confirm I did. She then pointed to each row in turn and asked me to blink again when I saw the line which contained that letter. This continued for my whole name and Emma's. During this laborious process I was drifting in and out of consciousness, but could still clearly demonstrate that I fully understood what to do. That weekend, when Mum went home for a brief interval in Burscough, she set about making me the blink chart that I have mentioned before, and which became so invaluable. She had found an example in Kate Allatt's book, so copied it on the computer and stuck it onto a cardboard cereal packet. It was colour-coded and had been lovingly manufactured.

Mum and Dad came in one day during the following week and proudly presented it to me. They asked what I wanted to talk about; it meant Mum and Dad could talk about something they knew I was interested in and it was a real breakthrough for all of us. I spelt out Paul and Tina's names. It was the first time I had been able to express any more than a yes or a no for weeks. Mum and Dad gave me a brief précis about how they were coping, and then the conversation returned to me. Next, I spelt out E-M-M-A; I already knew how she was, because she was with me every day, but I was on a roll. Dad, choking back emotions, said how she was coping wonderfully and that they had really gained another daughter. Any expression of emotion was too much for me and I became inconsolable, which forced a conclusion to the conversation.

Mum and Dad were with me every day at first and then every week thereafter, staying for a few days each visit. They both seemed to adopt their own unique roles. My dad used to feed me and give me drinks, whereas my mum was in charge of writing down the long string of letters I was indicating in her prayer journal, which she always carried. Mum also took it upon herself to massage my hands for what seemed like hours to relieve my spasticity. It was the only thing they were able to do in order to ease my suffering, so they took their jobs really seriously. It seemed whenever I needed to eat or drink, someone would have to have a very good reason why they might be better than my dad for him to relinquish his responsibility! As for Mum's prayer journal, it contained long lists of bizarre spellings as I failed to use the chart correctly or my dyslexia got the better of me.

I left the four-bedded bay for the first time in my wheelchair five weeks after my stroke to have a tour of the ward. It was a Tuesday and the excursion had been planned with my physio team for a few days. Paul happened to be visiting. The expedition only lasted ten minutes, after which I was exhausted and ready to go back to bed; however, it was considered a really big achievement and Paul was excited to be present. A week or so later, Tina was visiting and on hearing about my good time with Paul, she was looking forward to witnessing her own significant progress to share with the rest of the family. She came to afternoon visiting, but that morning I had had a severe panic attack and spelt out to Emma 'I'M DYING!', asking her to stay with me instead of going to work, so when Tina arrived I was not in the jovial mood she had hoped for.

I was in rehab when Paul said he had met a girl and wanted to bring her to visit. My desire to make a good impression was useless now, but it seemed important to Paul, so I hid my humiliation and said she could come down. Katie learned my communication chart almost immediately and we were able to chat. Paul seemed proud of both her manner and also my effort to make as best of an impression as I could. A whirlwind romance followed, and Katie and Paul were engaged and married just a few months later. I used to joke it was because Paul was driving my Mercedes that he finally attracted a girlfriend.

At Paul and Katie's wedding, just a year after I had the stroke, I was best man. I recorded my speech on video a week prior to the wedding and my friend subtitled my words for me so we could just play the video on the day itself. I had been planning the speech for months and Emma and my speech therapist were the only people who knew what I was going to say. We practised it for a while in all my speech therapy sessions before recording it. The speech elicited a mixture of laughter and tears from the guests; just what I had hoped for. It was strange to talk about the life Paul and I had shared before my stroke. It still seems strange that Katie, now being such a close family member, never knew me before the stroke. I used to be so professional and confident, and yet now I am so emotionally fragile. I sometimes feel more comfortable with friends and family who knew me before. When I remain quiet whilst everyone is discussing, they know it is my speech impeding me from contributing, rather than me having a lack of opinion on the subject. People who knew me before also know how out of character it is for me to allow any unguarded emotion to show. I often wonder how people perceive me now, if they never knew the old me, and this really destroys my confidence.

My family now, of course, includes Emma's parents. Four years before my stroke, I had boldly asked Emma's dad, David, for his blessing for me to assume responsibility for Emma's wellbeing by asking her to be my wife. I obviously recognised that Emma was quite a catch, but felt I could really offer something to her too. Just four years later I was unable to care for Emma whatsoever, and it seemed the roles had been reversed. It was important that I was able to temporarily hand back responsibility for Emma's wellbeing, not just to my family but also to Pam, Emma's mum, and David, who had successfully done the job for twenty-three years prior to our marriage. Emma relied quite heavily on her mum and dad at first and therefore, as I was her biggest responsibility, they gave us both a lot of support.

It is unusual to have someone speak about their dad

with such high regard and honour as Emma does. I was aware that at first I faced an almost impossible task as the other man in Emma's life. David and I possessed almost opposite temperaments; my personality was very much to act first and ask questions later, a bit like a bull in a china shop, whilst on the other hand David would be meticulously reflective before doing anything. In that sense we were chalk and cheese. However, Emma seemed to recognise common characteristics between us.

Just a month before my stroke, my granddad died, just days before his ninetieth birthday, leaving my grandma a widow. I was able to talk at the funeral and although I was upset, I managed to remain collected and deliver a tribute the way I wanted. Since my stroke, times and places of high emotions leave me without any control and my composure at any sort of sentimental event is almost non-existent. When I had my tracheostomy out and could begin to make sound, towards mid-December, we rang Grandma, and although I couldn't speak, I was able to grunt to confirm my presence. I did not know it then, but that was the last time I would speak to Grandma, because on New Year's Eve I got a message from Emma that Grandma's oxygen saturation was just mid-seventies and did I know what that meant? Of course I knew what it meant, and a few moments later the inevitable phone call came through. What really struck me about that last conversation with Grandma was that far from being a frail old lady, overwhelmed by circumstances, she was calm and utterly convinced I was going to be OK.

Growing up around my grandparents, we were also very close to my aunty Heather and my uncle Richard and my cousins, Robbie and Amy. Robbie studied sound production in Guildford, whereas Amy studied psychology at Edinburgh University and afterwards went on to work for the Christian charity, CAP – CAP seeks to advise and support people in managing their debt and helping families make a fresh start. One of our first holidays following the stroke was spent with Heather and Richard in their beautiful home just outside the Lake District. They seemed to have organised a full itinerary for us, and we were able to share their company when we went on days out.

Our families have always been close because that was just who we were, but following my stroke we couldn't have imagined the importance of having such an intimate family bond. Their support has been invaluable to Emma and me. I don't know how any couples could cope with such a trauma without such a caring family network who can share the burden.

Chapter 10

Friends

When I spoke to other people who had had a head injury, I heard stories of how previously close friends had become more distant as they found coping with the disability too difficult. Thankfully, I discovered the opposite. My previous friends were just as close, and former acquaintances had become companions. Many people used to visit me on various nights, but some people seemed to develop regular slots. Every other Tuesday, Peter would visit. Peter was a dental technician in Dudley, but by coincidence we had met on holiday in Barcelona, when Emma and I were dating. It turned out that because I didn't do any braces myself, I referred my patients to a specialist orthodontic practice and that practice happened to use Peter's laboratory to make the appliances; so many of my patients were walking around with Peter's work in their mouths, and neither of us knew each other. Peter was also trained in sports massage, and so after my stroke he massaged my arms and legs every time he came, to help reduce stiffness. Almost three years on, Peter still visits on alternate Tuesdays and continues to massage my limbs, and I try to offer some help with his course to become a clinical dental technician.

On a Wednesday, it was Ben's night; I had known Ben for a number of years through church, but we had been little more than acquaintances. During the time when I was recovering initially, Ben used to come and sit by my bed and read books from the Bible. Our friendship developed and Ben used to read various books to me, and when I improved my communication we were able to chat a bit. He also has a Masters in theology, so we are able to discuss things relevant to the theology course I later began to take. It's funny that he now writes critical appraisals for some of my lecturers! Ben has the dubious honour of being close enough for me to express the frustrations I usually keep just below the surface, when I'm not around family. Ben has the impossible task of sometimes helping Emma with DIY, a task I normally have quite strong opinions about, and want to be done in a very specific way. Ben is thick-skinned enough to diplomatically but forcefully answer back, but in a compassionate way that doesn't further escalate my frustration. Ben is single and about to turn forty. He comes for dinner every Wednesday, and we sometimes take trips out.

Andrew used to visit me on Sunday nights. A few years ago, we lived around the corner from each other and formed a prayer partnership, meeting every Tuesday morning, praying over shared breakfast. Andrew and his wife, Becky, used to run the youth department at church when I first became a leader. They were a huge influence on me growing as a Christian, and I had the honour of driving for their wedding; it was really special to spend forty-five minutes with them when normally guests only see a bride and groom for a few moments during the special day. We had first visited their twin daughters when they were less than a day old; they were tiny and delivered by Caesarean section. I remember holding Lucy in the palm of my hand, and struggle to believe they are grown-up little girls now. In more recent years they moved to the other side of the city, so we disbanded the prayer partnership but remained close friends. Andrew also brought his family to visit me on that first Christmas Day in 2011, and still comes on Sundays, as well as bringing Becky, Jessica and Lucy to visit me and, probably more importantly, our fish!

Monday night was always Harry and Dan's night. Dan and I met on our first day at Birmingham University as we were in the same halls of residence, and with us both starting a degree in dentistry, we immediately formed an acquaintance. During our Freshers' Week, we spent hours eating peanut butter and jam on toast, contrasting how we had lived our lives so far. Dan had attended a private boarding school. I suppose I had a bit of a chip on my shoulder, having only been to a comprehensive. However, Dan's work ethic was excellent, in contrast to mine, and he certainly sold the idea of a private education for those who can afford it. Two years later, I met Harriet (Harry) in a bar where dental students used to congregate. She was a year below, and we began talking about climbing. It was a hobby I used to pursue when I was younger and involved with scouting. Harry climbed with the university once a week, and invited me along to try it. We became climbing partners and great friends. Dan later joined the partnership, and the three of us used to climb on a Monday night after work. Emma encouraged Harry and Dan to visit, even when I was in intensive care. When my condition was more stable, Dan and Harry resumed our normal Monday night get-together, but now it was at the hospital rather than the climbing wall. Part of their visit would involve professionally cleaning my teeth because it was being done so poorly by the carers, if they remembered to do it at all. Otherwise we would just sit, chat, laugh and sometimes read.

Dan kindly preloaded some audio books he thought

I might enjoy onto an old iPod, and brought it in for me to listen to when there was no one visiting. Shortly after my stroke, one Monday night Dan was unable to come, so Harry came with her fiancé, Peter, although they only stayed for a short time because they had to leave early. To ensure I wasn't bored, they put the iPod onto Steve Jobs' autobiography. The story of the creation of Apple spanned over an audio book, totalling twenty-four hours play-time. They put my headphones in and merrily set it playing before leaving. I enjoyed the story for about an hour and then realised my predicament. To any nurses who looked my way I seemed to be enjoying my iPod, so they didn't disturb me, and with my tracheostomy still fitted, I couldn't make a sound to get attention. I fell in and out of sleep while it droned on, only being set free once the iPod battery ran out. It was months before I could tell them the true horror of what led to me never wanting to listen to another word about Steve Jobs and the creation of Apple; it has since become a joke between the three of us, with Dan and Harry teasing me about it.

I misjudged what was sustaining our friendship, thinking that it was dependent on what I could offer. I never felt that a friend of mine should need to give something in return, but for whatever reason I was very insecure about having a friendship to which I could no longer give valuable input. In my weakness,

I also felt unable to support Emma, but Harry and Dan did what they could to step in on my behalf. At the beginning, Harry texted or rang Emma most nights to check that she was OK, and also made extra portions when cooking so that she knew Emma was eating healthily. There was also a time when Emma bumped her car and was unable to use it to go to work or visit me. Dan's wife, Beth, had just had their first child and wasn't really driving much. So they lent Emma their car; it was a beautiful black sporty Mercedes. Emma was driving around like a queen for a week.

It was impossible to ever repay the friendship I received from Dan and Harry, but in April Harry was getting married and it was one of my goals, set months earlier, to be able to attend. I had known Harry for years, and now she had met Peter, who had become a very good friend too, and it seemed important to go to the wedding to show how happy I was for them both.

A few weeks before the wedding, my CHC nurse said I shouldn't be travelling as far as Buckinghamshire, which just made me more determined to go. So we hired a wheelchair-accessible vehicle and with the help of a friend, planned the drive down for the ceremony and then back to the hospital. On the morning I took a travel sickness tablet, but by the end of the road, I was violently sick; the combination of acute nerves and motion meant that the sickness continued until we reached the motorway. An hour and a half later, we frequented once again the bumpy A roads and I was sick a fourth time. We arrived at the church with just enough time for me to change into my shirt and recover from the traumatic journey. I recognised many of the other guests as they began to arrive. I had known them professionally. I felt incredibly insecure meeting them like I was, but I had made it. The ceremony was great, and after it finished I was really keen to slip away and get back to the hospital as soon as possible. As I tried to make a swift exit, Harry rushed over and we both burst into tears, but she was insistent that we had our photo taken before I was able to finally make my escape.

A bit later it was Dan's daughter's christening at Dan's old school near Reading. When Seren was being born, I got two very unexpected visits from Dan: one on Christmas Eve, when Beth was in labour but not due for hours, and again on Christmas Day, when I was given the good news, and Beth was just trying to get some sleep. The women's maternity hospital was a few hundred yards away from where I was on the stroke unit, and I think Dan just needed to get away.

The christening was another opportunity for me to put a small amount back into our friendship. I knew it would be attended by many of Dan's school friends, and although I got along with them very well, I had always felt inferior when they visited and this was going to be a hundred times worse. They had all grown up together at boarding school, and so they shared a wealth of experiences with each other that I knew nothing about. Emma drove this time, and it took about two hours to get there. When we arrived we couldn't see any wheelchair spaces, so we had to park on the gravel car park; we must have looked a real pair trying to get across the car park with my wheelchair getting stuck, and Emma trying to push wearing high heels.

As we entered a corridor leading to the chapel, I could hear lots of strangers and I was dreading going into the main building. As I rounded the corner, I saw Dan's sister and her husband; I had forgotten they would be there, yet just a few months earlier they had come to our house so Dan's brother-in-law could play his harp especially for Emma and me. He was a professional harpist, having recently played and toured with the pop star, Sting. Although I didn't know them especially well before the stroke, we got along very well and it was good to see a pair of friendly faces. I knew the worst trauma of the day was going to be eating after the service in front of dozens of people who I knew, but wasn't close to. Not only would Emma have to feed me, which was undignified enough, but I would be eating with my mouth open and also, no doubt, be coughing on my food. I stuck myself in the corner and tried to concentrate on my chewing and not who was watching. After it was done, I felt relieved that it was another goal achieved.

I should also mention Steve, with whom I first became acquainted during the men's walks organised by our church. Steve is a little bit older than Emma and me, but still quite young at heart. When Steve unexpectedly expressed an interest in coming skiing with Emma, myself and another friend, we were able to get to know him better. I recall a meal we had during this ski trip. We were eating Thai green curry, which had been mass catered and kept deliberately bland to suit all tastes. A jar of chilli sprinkles had been placed on each table to spice things up if individuals wanted to. Every time Steve glanced across the table, I added a few more chillies to his meal. This became more and more brazen as the meal went on, but Steve was so engrossed in conversations and seemingly enjoying his dinner so much, he was unaware. At the end of the meal, a few people innocently commented about how the meal was nice but a bit bland. Steve couldn't agree less. He said how he thought it was quite tasty. Emma and I were inconsolable with laughter and Steve really wanted to know what the joke was. Being in fits of laughter around Steve was nothing unusual; we would either be laughing at his account of certain misfortunes he'd had, or at his jokes.

Another time, in the summer just before my stroke, a large group of us met to stay in a hotel while we attended our friends' wedding. I was sharing with Emma, and Steve was sharing with our mutual friend, John, in the next room. Steve had taken himself off to bed a little bit earlier than the rest of us, so when he awoke to knocking at the door, he slipped out of bed, flicked open the door and jumped quickly back into bed. Steve chooses to sleep naked, so he was keen to get back under his covers as quickly as possible. A man came stumbling into the room, visibly drunk, and Steve was a little bit shocked at the apparent behaviour of John, who we all had hitherto considered a little more reserved. As the man stumbled towards the bathroom, Steve looked across and, to his horror, saw John's head on the pillow in the bed next to him. Realising he had just let a drunken stranger into their bedroom, he had to act. Because it was dark in the room, he thought his modesty would be protected enough to usher the man out the door, as liberating their room had just become the primary concern. He managed to encourage the man towards the door, but just before he exited the room, the stranger flicked the switch by the door. Steve was momentarily standing in the room with all the lights on, in his birthday suit!

Steve visited every week when I was in hospital, but being a bit more of a free spirit, I never knew when he was coming; he would just turn up. This was great because he was able to meet many of my other friends, and visit when I wasn't otherwise expecting anyone. He used to ask questions and get me to blink a reply; he would then compose some instructions for my family so they knew what I wanted, but he used to add other things so no one knew what I had actually said and what was made up! These instructions were usually hilarious and concluded by warning that my choice could change in the 'blink of an eye'. He also got to know the man in the bed next to me, who was quite lonely and rarely had visitors of his own. They used to talk about football, and when he left hospital to go to a care home, Steve began visiting him there. During our friendship, he met Nina, his beautiful fiancée, and she quickly became our friend too. They have a very happy baby boy, who seems to smile constantly. Just before he was born, we managed to share a holiday with them in Cornwall in August 2013, which of course was full of laughs.

There were hundreds of people who came to visit during my time in hospital. I always had far more visitors than anyone else. When I came home we had a party to say thank you to friends who had been consistently faithful in visiting us during my time in hospital. There were over ninety who came, and this didn't even include family; sadly, we couldn't invite everyone who had visited because we simply didn't have space.

I cannot overstate how much my friendships have meant to Emma and me. It is still of huge interest to hear how everyone else's lives are continuing, but it can be painful to know that they are realising some of the dreams that I had hoped for but cannot now grasp. I am really aware that most of my friends do not have a significant disability themselves, and so I think it's hard for them to fully understand the pain, frustration and feelings of despair I face daily, but I am comforted that they still do all they can to empathise with me. I often wonder whether my friends have stuck by me because they valued me so much as a friend before the stroke or whether I am still able to contribute to our friendship.

Chapter 11

And Then...?

- by Barbara

'For I know the plans I have for you,' declares the
LORD, 'plans to ... give you hope and a future.'
(Jeremiah 29:11)

At the time of writing this chapter, two years had
passed since Andy's devastating stroke. He spent a
total of ten months in hospital, three and a half months
on the stroke ward at the acute hospital, and six and
a half months in the neuro-rehabilitation unit. After
being allowed out of hospital for a few day visits, Andy
finally came home permanently on 2 September 2012
to an amazing welcome from over ninety local friends
who had faithfully visited, supported and prayed
throughout the darkest of days. For Andy, it was the
equivalent of being released from prison, back to the
real world and the freedom to be part of it.

The time spent in hospital and rehabilitation was a

rollercoaster ride of tears and laughter, setbacks and progress, doubt and faith. For Andy, there were times of great frustration, depression and fear, as the quality of care and level of therapy given varied tremendously and progress was extremely slow. During the darkest of times, Andy would cry inconsolably, and desperately seek assurance that he would get better. He laboriously spelled out, blinking one letter at a time, asking, 'ARE YOU SURE GOD WILL HEAL' 'I DOUBT IT EVERY DAY', but a few weeks later was telling us, 'I CAN ENDURE A LOT IF I HAVE HOPE'. Once, when Andy was alone, he was thoughtlessly and cruelly told he would have to go into a nursing home when he left hospital; in his weak and very vulnerable position this was absolutely devastating, and he pleaded, 'NO NURSING HOME'. We assured him that whatever it took or whatever it cost, we would never allow this to happen. We were all greatly reassured by Randy, a CHC nurse and a most gracious lady, that she would be submitting a 'very strong application' for further in-patient care until Andy was well enough to go home. We shared with Randy how as Christians we believed in the power of prayer and that our hope for Andy and Emma's future was in God's hands. She shared with us that she and her son had watched as thousands of football fans had prayed for Fabrice Muamba as medics fought to save his life on the pitch. She would never again doubt the power of prayer, and would do all she could to help. Just when we were all slipping into an abyss of doubt and depression, God had sent this gracious lady to reassure us of his love. God's timing was perfect, yet again.

Despite the continuing frustration and fear of being an in-patient, Andy now began to make plans for the future, to live at home, to buy a wheelchair-accessible car and redesign his computer and communication technology which he could control himself. Emma began taking Andy to private hydrotherapy sessions which Andy still enjoys today, and which have helped prevent his muscles completely seizing up.

Throughout his ten months' 'incarceration', there were many frightening and distressing times, especially at night, but during visiting times we were able to enjoy a good laugh. One man shared his joke book with Andy at night after visitors had left, and they had to be told off for making so much noise. He would also crack his own jokes, making Andy laugh as he was eating, catapulting food shrapnel across the ward! We would joke about the 'ice hat and gloves' put on Andy when his body was unable to control its own temperature, and about the pills crushed in thickened water because staff thought Andy couldn't swallow them whole; he spelled out: 'NO RANCID COCKTAILS'.

Andy's first time out of bed was to be pushed in a huge tilt-space wheelchair along the ward by his brother, Paul, the two of them laughing and joking loudly as Paul gave a running commentary on what they were passing along the way. 'On the right we have the cleaner's room,' etc.

One day Andy caused much hilarity himself by blinking out 'MYNIA ZA VUT' and looking towards the wife of the patient next to him. 'It doesn't make sense,' I protested, but he insisted I said it to the young wife. Andy was 'speaking' Russian, and Ingrid understood him perfectly. Most of the laughter, however, was when Andy and Emma shared private jokes, often finding the simplest things uproariously funny. Other patients and their relatives were amazed that Andy and Emma laughed so much, as they perceived Andy's plight to be so desperate. We were able to share our faith with them, explain that we believed God was in control of the situation, and that Andy would be healed.

We were to meet many inspirational people, many caring and dedicated professionals and many new friends throughout the months in hospital. There were many patients who, despite their own progressive neurological illnesses, considered Andy to be far worse off than themselves, and helped him when he was in distress and talked to him when he was alone. Yet they faced a very uncertain future as their illnesses gradually disabled them more and more. There were some nurses and therapists who gave Andy their time and attention, calling to see him off duty and giving him extra time in the physiotherapy gym. Other patient's visitors would call on Andy while in the hospital, including the five-year-old twins who came to talk to Andy when visiting their daddy. Little Joseph said he wanted to marry Emma, and was most upset that Andy already had!

Andy's and Emma's house was perfectly adapted to enable him to come home; amazingly, Andy had designed the extension and alterations to the ground floor himself before his stroke, and all the work was completed to his specifications whilst in hospital. There was very little which needed to be adapted to accommodate Andy's wheelchair, giving him access to all rooms including the downstairs wet room/ shower and the huge open plan kitchen/diner. The only difficulty was the upstairs bedroom, so Andy had to sleep in a 'hospital style' bed in the lounge; not ideal! Once again, Andy designed further alterations to accommodate a lift to the first floor, and found an internet company that would make a bed which would meet his needs and enable him to sleep with Emma in the upstairs bedroom.

There is storage space for all the specialist equipment which enables Andy to have therapy and exercise at home every day. With NHS therapy no longer offered, fortunately Andy is able to have two hydrotherapy sessions and a specialist neuro-physiotherapy session each week, all of which is privately funded. Thankfully, Andy's pension, allowances and insurances enable him to buy into these private therapy services; what happens to people who cannot afford to pay for therapy?

We are mindful that despite his severe disability and need of twenty-four hour care, Andy is in a far better position than most who have suffered similarly devastating illnesses. How many people languish in nursing homes after leaving hospital?

Research and medical journals tell us that brainstem stroke, leading to Locked-in syndrome is extremely rare, often undiagnosed in the initial acute phase and completely incurable. Many sufferers die within four months of onset (usually because their respiration is compromised by pneumonia), and those who survive are left with severe disabilities and little hope of living any sort of independent life. As muscles controlling swallowing are affected, the risk of aspirating food is a real threat, so patients may need feeding via a tube directly into the stomach. Speech may never be regained, so patients may be offered assistive communication technology (a computer which can be controlled by head movement or 'eye gaze') and a powered wheelchair if they can control it with their head. It is very rarely anyone is offered therapy after the first twelve months and many with Locked-in syndrome are denied the opportunity to make any significant progress in regaining mobility.

In the fourteen months since coming home, Andy's progress and achievements have been staggering, in part due to his determination to overcome his physical disability and regain some control of his life. He immediately ordered a new computer and, using a head mouse, was able to use inbuilt functions and software to access the internet, online banking, email and make 'Face Time' phone calls. It is so exciting when I am on the computer at home in Lancashire and an email, online chat or video call from Andy pops up on-screen. From Emma's point of view, the computer is a mixed blessing as Andy enjoys online shopping. The first Emma knows of his spending is when a parcel is delivered to the door!

Andy has also been able to write parts of this book himself on the computer by recording his memories of his time in hospital. His speech has improved to the point where he can say everything he wishes with minimal slurring, and this has enabled him to dictate huge chunks of this book and participate in conversation and discussions with family and friends. His aim now is to improve speech volume and speed, which are muscular problems, by regaining the ability to take deep breaths voluntarily (diaphragm control) and move his tongue and mouth more quickly. In the early days, speech and language therapists worked hard with Andy, and he has seen huge improvements in his ability to chew and swallow food. He can now eat most foods un-mashed and take liquids which are less thickened, as he is regaining voluntary control of his swallow.

The exercise and therapy sessions have kept his muscles loose and moving, but for most of the time he has been hindered by painful muscular spasms in his limbs. Spasticity was being controlled by the drug baclofen, a muscle relaxant, which Andy had to take orally in large doses, but it made him very tired. It was decided that fitting an 'intrathecal baclofen pump' would solve the problem, automatically pumping tiny doses of the drug into the spinal fluid and directly to the muscles in spasm. After waiting over six months, the pump was fitted, and within a week spasticity in the legs was gone and the arms were much improved. His therapists are supporting him in this, but also and more importantly helping him make 'new pathways' in the brain (taking messages from the brain to the limbs and making them move voluntarily.)

Andy has maintained a rigorous daily exercise/ therapy routine ever since coming home using electrical stimulation, a standing frame, an active/ passive therapy bike and SaeboFlex 'gloves'. The bike and the SaeboFlex were bought with money raised by friends who took part in sponsored events and raised £14,000 between them. It is very humbling but also really encouraging, receiving such kindness and practical help along with the support and prayers of thousands around the world.

When we are tempted to get disheartened or angry about Andy's plight, we need to remind ourselves that actually God is at the heart of the situation, that Andy is surrounded and protected by His love, and He 'is able to do immeasurably more than all we ask or imagine, according to his power that is at work within us' (Ephesians 3:20). We pray, trust and hope that Andy will continue to regain movement and speech, and achieve more independence, but that whatever the degree of physical healing, it will be to God's glory. From being a small child, Andy has always been very determined, strong-willed and stubborn; characteristics which have enabled him to overcome many obstacles and strive to do the best he can in every situation. This determination has probably helped him to deal with the traumas he has faced, and still motivates him to do all he can to improve his condition and the quality of life he shares with Emma. Doctors can give no hope of any healing or improvement, but we believe the words of Jesus who said, 'all things are possible with God' (Mark 10:27), and we continue steadfastly to place our hope and trust in Him, giving thanks for the many blessings showered upon us.

Chapter 12

Holidays

At first, just coming home in September 2012 was like the best holiday ever, but as the weeks passed it just became normal and I wanted a change of scenery. We went to visit my mum and dad in Burscough, but we really wanted to arrange a holiday away from places we knew, so we searched for a specialist hotel with the necessary mobility equipment and care. We found one in Blackpool, and although we weren't drawn to it because of its location or the on-site entertainment, we thought the hotel would provide a perfect base for us to explore the surrounding area. So in March 2013, we had our first holiday in over eighteen months. Blackpool was windswept and mostly closed because we had gone out of season, but we were able to take the tram along the coast and wheel back along the promenade. We found out that wheelchair users could apply for a free bus pass, which the trams would accept.

We booked a room for Emma and I and another one for my parents, and we asked the hotel to provide an hour and half of care each morning to help Emma. The hotel was quite a friendly place and the food was good. Many of the guests had psychological as well as physical disabilities, so I felt quite comfortable that I wasn't drawing unnecessary attention to myself. There was a programme of entertainment each night, which culminated in the headline act of the week, a drag queen who liked to include the audience in the show. Needless to say I chose to get an early night instead, or get out of the hotel and explore the few places which were open.

In the morning, when our carers arrived, we learned they were not employees of the hotel but simply agency carers whom the hotel had booked on our behalf. Learning this, we realised that if we went away somewhere there was nothing to stop us hiring an agency carer ourselves to help Emma with the morning routine. That was certainly an idea for the future. Whilst we were staying in Blackpool, we travelled to my aunt and uncle's house in Kirkby Lonsdale. We wanted to investigate the logistics of us staying there for our next holiday. As mentioned earlier, we did this a few months later.

One day, from Kirkby Lonsdale, we took a trip to the coast, where we went to the Midland Hotel in

Morecambe. They had a formal restaurant, and we enjoyed some cuisine whilst looking out to sea. I ordered a slow-cooked boeuf bourguignon with creamy mashed potatoes and French beans. The sauce was really rich and the beef so well cooked it slipped down my throat with ease! The whole experience was not half as bad as I expected, and the food was fantastic; the other diners were much more interested in their own meals and company than in me. This was the first time I had been to a restaurant since my stroke, and I enjoyed it so much that I promised myself and Emma that we would repeat the experience somewhere else when we got back to Birmingham.

Feeling confident, a few weeks later we ventured to the Elim Bible Week (an annual conference for the Elim Pentecostal denomination of churches) in Telford. The hotel adjacent to the conference centre had a hoist, so we rang up a local care agency to see if someone could come in and help as a one-off. Our night away was a real success, and we finished off the little getaway by visiting another restaurant. On our return home, we immediately booked another trip down to London on the train. This was a new challenge. Emma carried my big hiking rucksack with all of the stuff we needed for the weekend on her back so she could push me in the wheelchair. The train journey ran smoothly and we were able to relax. We stayed in another specially adapted hotel and used a local care agency. We found London transport very accessible; we were able to travel around on the buses and the river taxi. We had lunch at the O2 before going to see a West End show in the evening. We used the trip to meet up with Tina and Keith, who accompanied us to the show and then helped push me back to our hotel.

In the summer of 2013, my aunt and uncle also booked us a newly opened and specially adapted cottage in Looe, Cornwall. There was a huge bathroom and a lift which could lower me into the bath; a real treat I hadn't experienced for months! This time we took our friends Steve and Nina away with us for company and support, if necessary. On one of these days, we travelled out to the Eden Project. They had electric wheelchairs available for other disabled visitors to use, but I was unable to transfer into one without a hoist, so Emma and Steve took it in turns to push me around the steep slopes in the big biomes. For a short time in the afternoon, Emma and I went off alone so both couples could have some time to themselves. It was at this time that Steve was casually walking up a sloped path when he saw one of the electric wheelchairs careering out of control around a corner towards him! The chair left the pavement and Steve, understanding my own vulnerability and assuming the wheelchair user was equally helpless, leapt to action to save the person. As he lurched for the wheelchair, its inhabitant jumped out and turned around sheepishly. Steve was a bit annoyed. 'What a disgrace to disabled people,' he thought to himself as the man made his escape!

We'd got the bug for travelling. During the next few months we visited London another two times, and went twice to see our friends in South Wales, staying overnight in Cardiff.

The following spring, in May 2014, we decided to book ourselves a proper week's holiday in the furthest place south I dared to go: Jersey. We looked at potential holiday properties, but all those with their own hoist looked very clinical, more like a nursing home than a holiday apartment. We began to look for regular disabled access accommodation and hire our own equipment and carers to help with my morning routine. This plan turned out to be much more expensive than we expected, but not long after this, we learned that Emma had been left some money by her nan when she passed away, so we put the money towards our Jersey holiday and didn't worry about the expense. We also spoke to Paul and Katie about joining us for the week, and the four of us then began looking forward to it.

Even when I was well, I used to stress about travelling when I was going on holiday, but now I was unable to plan, and knowing Emma had always relied on me for organising, I was apprehensive. It must have been something in the Davies' genes, however, because my brother was every bit as organised as I would have been if I were well. Our journey went without a hitch, and preceded a wonderful holiday where we spent days walking the waterfront, eating at nice restaurants and seeing what Jersey had to offer tourists. We went to the war tunnels, which chronicled the lives of islanders living during the German occupation in the Second World War. We spent a day at the wildlife park, which was more like a sanctuary for endangered species rather than a zoo. And on one of our last days we went to a vineyard and signed up to a tour and wine tasting experience. On that holiday, I discovered I could drink wine without any thickener, provided I used a cocktail straw with a really narrow bore to give me as much control as possible. We brought home a bottle of red and white wine so I could enjoy it with my family and demonstrate my new skill. It was expensive staying in Jersey, but everything seemed to work well and the tourist destinations were efficient. We returned home agreeing that Jersey had been our best holiday post-stroke. On our return, knowing that I had coped with such a significant ferry crossing, we immediately threw caution to the wind and booked a week's cruise for the following May.

In July 2014, we travelled once again to Heather and Richard's and this gave us some more firsts, such as a trip to the Calvert Trust's Residential Outward Bounds Centre in the north of the Lake District. Heather and Richard had encouraged me to stay at the centre overnight, but I felt that I would be unable to talk and make friends, so I asked instead if I could just do some activities as a non-residential visitor. In the morning we opted to go sailing, and I was hoisted into a tri-marine yacht. There seemed to be very little forward planning about how to do this, but it transpired there wasn't a specific way, and instead the instructors just played around with various foam pads and straps to make me comfortable and secure. We went out on the lake for an hour or so and I sat soaking up the sun while the instructor sailed us back and forth. Previously I would have enjoyed the sheer thrill of making the yacht go as fast as possible. Now, however, being unable to control the yacht myself in any way, I gained enjoyment from simply taking in the views.

I concluded that with all such activities, a pleasurable adrenalin rush, which came from me relying on my own skill or wit to maintain my safety in the face of danger, was no longer achievable. If I was safely harnessed in place, why would I be afraid? Conversely, if there were any element of danger now, I knew I would have no control, which would be terrifying. In the afternoon we teamed up with another guest to go canoeing. The organisers rafted two canoes together to make things more stable, and the six of us went out onto the lake to explore. The young guest we shared that afternoon with was also in a wheelchair, but had the use of her arms and could talk. She was there with her carers, and Emma and I quizzed her all afternoon about living with a disability. She was staying in a cottage owned by the Calvert Trust, and we felt this would be something we could also do in the future.

Because of our hectic regime and many hours around the house, we have set ourselves the challenge of going away somewhere every month so we always have something to look forward to. Sometimes this will just be a trip up to Mum and Dad's, but we try to ensure there is always at least a night away each month. In addition to this escape, Emma and I have a date night each week where we find a local restaurant to sample. We have found many of the large hotels in Birmingham have excellent restaurants and are usually quiet midweek. They are perfect for what we are looking for.

Chapter 13

Regents

The stroke which devastated my life was isolated to a tiny but essential part of my brain called the pons; this is the bridge between the higher centres and the rest of my body. In theory, my cognition hasn't been affected in the slightest, and yet I could feel my brain beginning to become more dulled as the months passed by – maybe because I failed to use it except to watch daytime TV. During one visit to the rehab centre, a friend presented me with a self-modified Connect Four game, where I was required to name a letter to select where I wanted my counters to be put. In my emotionally labile state, I found winning impossible. Every time I got close to putting in a victorious piece, I would get excited and be unable to hide my delight, alerting the other player to their imminent defeat and allowing them to reconsider their move. However, these games of Connect Four seemed to wake my brain again. As time progressed, about eighteen months into my recovery, and with me being settled at home, my mind returned to the conundrum of how I could regain some of the mental sharpness I had previously enjoyed.

I considered lecturing again, but public speaking was not really an option; I also considered marking dental papers, but although I enjoyed teaching dentistry, probably one of the worst responsibilities I had was to mark my trainees' work; I hated it. It was about this time that Lynette, one of my friends, challenged me to consider what I would have done in my previous life, if I had had the time. I thought about that for a few days and concluded I would have enjoyed a theology course, just to be better informed in regards to the Bible.

At first, I dismissed this as silly and another thing I could never do. I could only use my head mouse to type about fifteen to twenty characters a minute at best, so a 2,000-word essay would be impossible, assuming I even knew what to say; I couldn't even read textbooks. I then wondered if I could just pay my fee and attend the lectures in order to challenge my thinking and enjoy the academic style of address. I began to look into it, speaking to staff members from Regents Theological College at the Elim Bible Week. I favoured Regents because of its links to the Elim denomination; some of my friends were alumni there and Stuart knew quite a few of the lecturers. With it being a reasonable commute from Birmingham, I had visited the college in the hills of West Malvern a few years earlier; I was instantly captivated by its surroundings. Of course, this stunning backdrop came at a price, with it being a sloped site on the side of a large, steep hill, making it one of the least appropriate locations from an accessibility point of view. In spite of all this, that was where I decided I wanted to go. I began by informally asking a few general questions and then, as time passed, they became more specific.

There was no doubt from initial conversation that the proposal was just as daunting to the administration team; they had never had a student in a wheelchair before, let alone someone with my additional challenges. Despite this, the team made every accommodation from the onset, from the initial site tour, where every possible logistic was considered, to the prospective interview, where two of the senior lecturers visited me at home so I could answer their questions more intelligibly. Even though my posture was relaxed in my recliner, I aptly dressed in a suit for the occasion, insisting to my carer, who was getting me ready, that he would have to consult YouTube and learn how to tie a double Windsor knot; I still considered a normal tie knot to be inappropriate for interviews! Things seemed to continue to slot into place.

Feeling more comfortable about how I would

navigate around the site, I was initially ecstatic to be offered a place. However, this elation was superseded by questions about how I would manage the academic side. The study support officer at the college explained how I should go about applying for funding for study aids. Emma and I attended a lengthy assessment in Birmingham, where various technologies and human support were considered to mitigate my various individual challenges. I already had my adapted computer, so the other most important support agreed was the provision of a study facilitator, who could not only attend lectures, but also support me at home for a full day a week. The college wisely recommended one of their former students, Sarah, to fill this role. It transpired that we had much in common. Sarah had already heard about my situation, when I initially had the stroke, and had been following my progress; she was also a close friend of Peter, as they had ministered together at a church in Dudley. She was a similar age to me and grew up in Birmingham. As it turned out, she had just taken on a minister-in-training role part time and happened to have Thursdays and Fridays off, which were the days timetabled for study for open learners. We hit it off straight away. By September 2013, I had been promised the help I needed and was able to enrol for the first year of a six-year part-time applied theology degree. Bizarrely, I was now not only officially retired and claiming my pension, but also a student, and I looked forward to being able to enjoy the benefits of these polar opposites.

We arrived late in the evening, ready for my first day at Regents. Emma and my carer had just enough time to unpack and assemble my hoist before they started on the usual nightly routine of tea and meds and getting me into bed. The room was perfect, wonderfully spacious with a huge accessible bathroom; much more like a hotel room than a typical student pad. The two single beds, which lay side by side, had plenty of room for the hoist to go under, were beautifully dressed and had fresh towels neatly laid out. Tea and coffee making facilities were also set up in the corner of the room. When in bed, I realised how much I missed just sleeping on a standard mattress rather than the noisy air one I was so used to. However, my intense apprehension of what the next few days would hold meant that I simply couldn't drift off, which further fuelled my anxiety; having a good night's sleep was paramount to me coping.

My first day as a student was intense to say the least, especially in comparison to my relatively sedate timetable at home. My alarm was set for 6:30 to ensure there was sufficient time to get ready before breakfast, which was served from 8 a.m. The canteen area was reasonably quiet as only freshers were timetabled for study days that week. Whilst tucking into their own breakfasts, the carer and Emma took it in turns to feed me. I tried to eat my bacon and eggs as neatly as I could, carefully concentrating on timing my swallow accurately, to avoid unnecessary spluttering and attention from other students. My tummy was knotted in sheer panic. My biggest fear for the day was that I would have an outburst of emotion in class and draw unnecessary attention to myself. My intense self-consciousness and nerves meant that when in new settings, I find it very difficult to maintain my composure.

Devotions started at 9 a.m. in the lecture theatre; all of the freshers, both full-time and open learners, were expected to attend. Emma and I crept in as discreetly as possible, despite the only wheelchair-accessible area being on the front row. There were probably about a hundred other students. You could spot the more mature, open learners amongst the residentials, who were mainly fresh from college. Jeff, one of the lecturers who had visited me at home, addressed the crowd warmly, attempting to put everyone at ease. Bracing myself, I was already aware that any moment he would be formally introducing me to the rest of the students. He made it clear that although I struggled in other respects, my intelligence was very much intact. I managed to remain calm and in a way felt relieved that the air had been cleared. Afterwards the other students greeted me. In fact, throughout those first few days I was warmly greeted and put at ease, with students introducing themselves and making the effort to find out about my background. Emma, of course, had to interpret my unintelligible speech, as I was upright in my wheelchair with little breath support.

Lectures commenced promptly after devotions in classroom five. This was the only accessible classroom so it would be my home for the next three days. There were about twelve other students in the group. I found it fascinating to learn of the different stories that had led them to Regents to study theology. One student was in the army, another a primary school teacher, another a vet. I did wonder, though, what these other students thought of me. I couldn't tell them of the fact that I too was once a high-flying professional; from observation of me now, I knew they would never guess this. A few times that day, the lecturer made a humorous comment; I would laugh along with the rest of the class, but it was unbecomingly overpowering and filled the room. In intense embarrassment, I laughed all the more. I was also unable to contribute in tutorials to class discussions. Whilst the other students reasoned with each other about theological ambiguities, I sat in silence, appearing to have very little opinion on anything. I can't imagine how unintelligent I must have appeared. I was especially concerned how others would view the presence of Sarah sitting next to me. If I began passing, would anyone think it was due to Sarah doing more than just supporting me? I batted off these negative thoughts; there was nothing I could do about them anyway.

Lectures continued into the late afternoon. Having lain dormant for so long, there was something quite magical about my brain being reawakened to the language of academia. Being Freshers' Week, events continued into the evening, so that by the end of the day, I had been in my chair for over twelve hours. It felt good to be back in my room, where I could let go of any apprehension about my emotions playing havoc. I lay in bed and reflected on the day. Although I was exhausted, there was a tremendous sense of achievement and satisfaction, but most of all, relief.

In those initial few days, I still had no idea how I would actually be able to do the various assessments necessary. Sarah and I, along with the lecturers who were setting the tasks, had to think hard about how we could keep these initial assessments as similar to the rest of my peers as possible. In the first module there was a writing test, where someone read out a series of ten sentences and we had to write these down using the correct spelling and grammar. The fairest way I could think of doing this was to wait until I was at home and have my study facilitator read them out while I typed them one character at a time using my head mouse. This simple, ten-minute quiz would take me about an hour and a half, but it would genuinely be my work. Another assessment we had during our first module was a reading comprehension. Because of my dyslexia, I was never very good at reading, but because my eyes were now affected, making it impossible to read the small text, the exercise was changed from a reading comprehension (which I would be terrible at) to a listening comprehension (one of my strengths).

During our first few days, I also volunteered to set up a Facebook group for all the open learners to be able to stay in touch. This was a small thing I was able to do, and if it was done correctly, it meant I could communicate just as well as anyone else. As it transpired, some members of the group were prolific at posting, and I had to be really keen to say something to embark on the task of typing with my head.

With the first study days over, we packed up the car and headed home. The stretch of motorway between Worcester and Birmingham would be one we would frequent regularly from now on, with me having to attend lectures every few weeks. With assignments set and continuous deadlines to meet, Sarah and I began our weekly study day at home on a Thursday, whilst Emma was at work. I always looked forward to these days. By the end of module one, I, to my amazement, was averaging a comfortable First, and although I had received no more help than was necessary to combat my disability, I was aware Sarah took some pride in how well I did, giving me the additional motivation of not letting someone else down.

As the year progressed, I continued to get high marks, proving to myself it wasn't just a fluke, and my attitude changed from merely wanting to attend lectures to being disappointed if I failed to get a First. When we had my end-of-year exams, it was a bit of a challenge to know just how I would be able to do it. In the end, the college staff converted an accessible room in the adjacent conference centre into an examination room so I could be hoisted onto the bed and dictate my exam answers in a supine position. I found revision for the exams almost impossible without help, so I often resorted to watching additional YouTube lectures on the subject, but I still entered the exam very unprepared. Using YouTube for revision was a gamble; there were tons of resources, but I didn't have any confirmation that they actually reflected what my lecturers were looking for; the reading list didn't recommend YouTube! I found the exams academically a real challenge, but did just enough to pass. I was relieved to have completed my first year.

Chapter 14

Faith

My disability is profound. I have no functional movement in my body below my neck, apart from my right thumb. I can barely speak, and even my eyes cannot focus properly. I have no ability to take deep breaths nor clear my throat voluntarily, and my power to select and control an appropriate emotion is almost non-existent. About the only two functions that still work properly are my hearing and the reasoning part of my mind. This has left me with more reasons to question my faith than most people, but God has left me with a brain capable of finding some hope amongst the despair.

In the first chapter of this book I referred to a drive for "a little bit more". I have it, and know others have it, but I believe everyone does to some extent. For some people it's just a dream that motivates them to buy a lottery ticket, for others it's a driving force to work hard and achieve more. Sadly, for some it's something which fuels ambition at the expense of honesty or integrity. Finally, for some people, the dissatisfaction they feel by not gaining this "little bit more" or the ebbing away of the belief they will ever achieve it, can cause depression and despair. This feeling doesn't seem to recognise status, or previous achievement. No matter where someone is, their biggest desire is for just a little bit more.

When I was well, I wasn't seriously motivated by dreams of fame or fortune, but just a little bit more money, a little more free time, and perhaps a slightly better car.

Now I find myself motivated just as strongly, not to be well, but to just be able to talk, chew and swallow, and perhaps use an electric wheelchair. It occurred to me that people who may have broken their necks (something I used to consider was as bad as it gets) may have these abilities, but are probably far from satisfied and want a little bit more themselves, not realising that what they have would be someone else's dream. Similarly, there are almost certainly people who would look at my life and see all the blessings I have compared to them, and naturally desire it. So although I am very dissatisfied with my life the way it is, I am not going to spurn my life and therefore disrespect someone else's dream.

Another belief I hold is that we as humans have a real spiritual enemy; some call him the devil, which I don't find helpful because of the images of red-horned creatures with a tail and pitchfork that spring to mind. But I believe his intention is to bring people to despair and away from their relationship with God. I don't think he can directly do this to Christians, but he can cause hurt, pain and suffering which can result in despair. Therefore, I believe my life can be affected by the actions of the enemy in regard to pain and suffering. But it's my faith and trust in God that prevents this pain and suffering leading to despair. So although my life is much harder and less agreeable than I would like, I believe the actions of the enemy in my life have fundamentally failed.

It seems to me that many people have an awareness of God, that He cares specifically for them, but this is often a purely emotional experience; for example, some say that they feel a real sense of peace during collective worship. These experiences can be real enough to sustain a Christian's faith for a time, but what happens when the trauma is so great that it causes these experiences to cease? If a person is depressed or they have a despairing situation, can their faith be sustained purely by memories of these experiences, if they don't continue? Larry Christenson says that 'There is great temptation to fall into sin' in these seasons but that we can 'experience ten times the spiritual growth' when we continue to cling to the Lord as when we go along simply in an easy time. He explains that anyone can do that. Christenson continues: 'God expects us to live in harmony with His will, even though we don't have the good feeling that makes it easy.' (Larry Christenson, *The Renewed Mind: Becoming the Person God Wants You to Be*, Bloomington, MN: Bethany House, 2001.) This was certainly my experience, and if I was going to have to cling to God, I needed a more rational and reasoned faith to be able to maintain my convictions. In this chapter I want to align some of these reasoned thoughts, which may prove useful when experiencing God seems impossible.

How was the world created?

In simple terms, I just don't know! The Bible begins with the assertion, 'In the beginning, God created the heavens and the earth' (Genesis 1:1). And science estimates that the universe is 13.8 billion years old and started with a big bang. My first conclusion is that these two assertions are not mutually exclusive. Prior to the 1960s, scientists believed the universe had always been there. This was in conflict to Christians, who insisted there was a beginning. Professor Stephen Hawking, however, explained that the previous assertions were based primarily on philosophy rather than any real science, and he was able to show that there was a beginning; there now seems little disagreement over this. There is some uncertainty about what happened next; namely, did evolution play a part?

The idea of evolution has been dismissed out of hand by many Christians, although I fail to see how proof of evolution is disproof of God, just as understanding about gravity isn't a stumbling block to faith. Sir Isaac Newton, who first described gravity, said, 'Gravity explains the motions of the planets, but it cannot explain who sets the planets in motion.' Having said that, I do not believe evolution is a very likely mechanism for advancing life. Charles Darwin discovered that a finch's beak evolved through natural selection to allow it to be better suited to the environment. This discovery has been observed many times since then to show how an individual species can evolve to better suit its environment. However, evolution between species has remained only a theory and cannot be evidenced. Therefore, I think the theory requires far too much of a leap of faith to conclude that a one-cell organism can accidentally evolve into a complex human without any divine help whatsoever. In contrast to my faith, which can sustain the very unlikely possibility that evolution could one day be proved, an atheist must cling to evolution as being the only possible explanation.

What causes suffering?

Once again I simply don't know. However, I can see that

people's actions lead to and cause the majority of pain and suffering. For example, a husband who is violent to his family may find later in life that he is suffering by being separated from the love of his wife and children. There is a direct cause and effect whereby his violent actions have led directly to his hardship. Moreover, a person suffering pain whilst recovering in hospital after being attacked won't have any difficulty attributing their suffering to someone else's actions. C.S. Lewis, in The Problem with Pain, said that this type of cause and effect could account for 80 per cent of suffering.

However, there is a minority of suffering to which there still seems to be no reasonable explanation, and in these cases we simply have to accept it, but we should try to minimise the majority of suffering over which we have control.

What do you believe is truth, when even Christians cannot agree?

One thing I am certain about is the existence of God, and that He cares about moral issues and has an opinion, which defines ultimate truth. I need to rely on my interpretation of scriptures, along with other people's interpretations. Where there is a clear consensus, we can be fairly sure the interpretation directly mirrors God's actual thoughts. When a consensus cannot be found and two groups of people have read the same scriptures but interpreted them differently, I cannot be confident my interpretation was right and theirs was wrong.

When a person who also believes in the supremacy of God's will differs in their views about what that will is, I need to approach the topic with much more humility about my own views. If a person doesn't recognise the supremacy of God and chooses to use human argument in order to make a point about moral issues, I'm inclined to take it less seriously. In issues that affect me, I tend to act in a way that I honestly believe God wants. Where the issue affects others, I can only commit to a position that God has an opinion, and I would follow it, but I cannot stubbornly assert my own interpretation.

Why can't I feel God?

If a person often has their spiritual needs met by what they feel, a cessation in these feelings can lead to fear and a sense of abandonment by God. We know that when an individual loses one of their senses, the others sometimes become heightened; for example, a blind person might have more acute hearing. As individuals, we are mind, body and soul, and sadly when one of these is attacked, the others don't necessarily get stronger but may also consequently suffer. If a person is depressed (suffering in their mind) or severely disabled (suffering in their body), it's not a surprise that the other elements suffer as well, meaning that God's Spirit may be communing with our spirit but the soul is too poorly to experience it.

Why do certain things have to happen?

I started watching past episodes of the BBC television series, Jonathan Creek. For those that do not know, each episode follows a very similar format. At the beginning, a crime is committed with apparently absolutely no plausible explanation, and we are, for whatever reason, sure that whatever has happened is not possible, and yet those who follow the programme know that Jonathan will come up with a reason for how it was done. During the programme, there are clues allowing us to understand that certain things are relevant to the final explanation, but we must wait until the end to understand what was really happening. It is impossible to predict what the final explanation will be. It seems a very good analogy for life in general. Things happen for which there is simply no explanation, but like the TV series, the Bible (re)assures us that there is an explanation; we just don't know what it is! During life, we get a sense of what is relevant to the final explanation, but we must wait until the end to find out why.

How can a Christian always be blessed?

Joseph is quite a well-known character from the Old

Testament, especially after a musical written about his life (Joseph and the Amazing Technicolor Dreamcoat). In the beginning of his story, he is quite a successful young man and it's clear to see God's blessing over his life, but suddenly he is sold into slavery; his life changes immediately, and now any blessing from God is harder to see. However, if we consider the outcome for people who are lying in the bottom of a pit, surrounded by murderous brothers who want them dead, it's truly remarkable that at that moment slave traders pass by and Joseph escapes with his life and remains faithful to God.

Later on in the story, we hear how Joseph's situation has become even graver as a prisoner in Egypt; there is no evidence of God's favour. Yet even now Joseph isn't just a prisoner; he is in charge of all the other captives and continues to remain faithful. I recognise that compared to most people, and especially my friends and family, my situation is pretty dire. However, when I compare myself to other people with brain injuries, I am truly fortunate. I own my own beautiful home, I am married, and we go on holidays a few times a year. There are countless blessings that I can recall from my life, and it isn't over yet! I have often wondered what I would be willing to give up in order to be healed, if it were possible to trade my suffering for another forfeit. I have come to the conclusion that my marriage, the closeness of my family, my faith and a hope for a better future one day are things I'm not willing to negotiate on, and I would rather stay as I am than compromise any of the above.

How can God have my best interests at heart?

In 2007, we took a group of teenagers away to a Christian holiday park for a few days. Stuart also brought along his family. One night we arranged to go out after dark for a hill walk. During the evening, Lydia (Stuart's youngest daughter) wanted to be involved with her two older brothers, but a night-time ascent up a hill was in no way appropriate for a six-year-old. Rather than reacting like a spoilt child who was not getting her way, she just sobbed, begging her dad to let her come along. It seemed this otherwise kind father was being unbelievably cruel on this occasion. Although everyone else understood it was sensible that she was to stay at the chalet, there was simply no way to make Lydia understand it was anything except cruel. I don't imagine either Stuart or Lydia still remember that night, but it has remained in my mind as an example of how our heavenly Father could love us and still appear unbearably cruel.

Does my situation still cause anger?

Since my stroke three years ago, friends, family and,

of course, I have expressed a lot of anger towards God for apparently not thinking about a more rapid healing. It occurred to me that this anger is actually quite a strong declaration of faith. There is no point getting angry with a God you are sure doesn't exist, and you must believe God is intricately involved enough to hear your anger when it's about one person on the planet of 7 billion. It is actually much darker when the anger ceases, because the events of life just seem so random.

Would I be better off dead?

From a Christian perspective, quite possibly I would. The Bible says, 'to live is Christ and to die is gain' (Philippians 1:21). So, do I therefore think that assisted dying should be legalised in order for me to escape this life and experience 'gain'? In my case, I feel I am more of a contributor than purely a burden, so my answer would be no. However, some people do not have that esteem and life can simply be an unbearable torture. It is difficult to see past the obvious compassion a person would feel for someone, where a person just wants help to end their suffering. But in agreeing to this, you inevitably agree with the person's assertion that their life is worthless. The more people who share this view – that the life is not valuable – inevitably begins to devalue the lives of people with similar conditions or even worse. The knowledge that society is beginning to value how worthwhile a life is could leave a sufferer with additional questions about the value of their own life.

***

In this chapter I have tried to explain how my faith has not only been sustained, but also how my thoughts have served to reassure and possibly strengthen my convictions. Three years ago, my family faced an impossible decision. The doctors, giving a purely scientific prognosis, said the damage to my brain was permanent and profound and I would only ever be able to blink, and it might be kinder to turn off the ventilator there and then. The other advice my family received was from Christians, who suggested it wasn't all over, and God could repair the brain and one day I would walk. Three years later, my progress probably wouldn't cause any sceptics to believe in God, but it doesn't endorse the doctors' scientific view either. Now I face an ongoing decision; knowing the doctors were wrong, I could, nevertheless, trust their judgement now or I could continue believing the claims of the Bible. If my faith turned out to be unfounded, I would have lived my life with hope and when I died, it would be an unconscious death and I couldn't regret it.

However, if I lived pursuing only pleasure and satisfaction, I could die having missed the most important decision of my life. The pursuit of pleasure and satisfaction in my situation, as opposed to many in our society, is futile and I only face despair and then die without God. So my decision to continue my faith is both rational and inevitable.

Chapter 15

Emma's Story: Part 1

Andy's book was complete. On sending the manuscript in its initial stages to publishers, their feedback was unanimous; they wanted to hear from me. I had, on several occasions, pondered what my side of the story could add but, to be brutally honest, was unsure how much I could comfortably divulge. To share the full context of our journey together, pre-and post-stroke, I would need to allude to some of my own brokenness. Without so doing the story of our mutual support of one another and God's sustaining grace could not be fully told.

I know indeed there have been countless comments of how strong, even stoic, I have been to cope with the whole ordeal. However, ordinarily this would never have come naturally. Despite my having a happy and stable childhood, being outgoing, popular and even a little cheeky at times at school, things began to change dramatically when I was around thirteen. I can't explain it, except that with the onset of my teenage years, and with my hormones kicking in, I was becoming a very anxious young lady, particularly in regards to whether I matched up to what a good 'Christian' should be.

To counteract the anxiety, I tried to perform perfectly or avoid situations. By the time I was seventeen, I had spiralled into a depth of despair I had never before experienced. I finally sought medical intervention and was prescribed anti-depressants. Surprisingly, the tablets worked quickly and were wonderfully effective – maybe a little too effective – and I swung from a place of being suicidal to being abnormally happy and carefree. It was difficult to sleep because I couldn't switch off my racing thoughts. As days and weeks passed, my mood continued to rocket but was interspersed with moments of severe irritability and frustration. Family rallied round to try to support me from home, but finally it was decided that I needed to be treated in an adult mental health ward. During my stay there, I would return from the extreme high to the depths of despair that I had experienced only weeks earlier. At just seventeen I was given the devastating diagnosis of bipolar disorder, a condition where, without proper treatment, I would transition from depression to elation.

On discharge, I was still very poorly and extremely

depressed, but I began to stabilise relatively quickly and by the following September I was able to recommence my A-levels before moving on to university and embarking on a successful career in teaching in the Further Education sector. When I say stable, this is a relative term. Coming to terms with this part of me was not easy in the slightest; I still had episodes of depression and anxiety where, at times, I neared crisis points. I accepted that I would have to take medication and this was helpful, but equally I also grew in my faith, accepting some key Christian truths about God's grace and unconditional love and acceptance: that I am right with God not on the basis of anything I do or don't do, but because of the finished work of Christ on the cross.

I met Andy at the tender age of twenty-two. I wasn't looking to meet anybody; quite the contrary, I thought that with all the 'stuff' I was still battling with, it would be a long time before I would be ready to settle down. So, I admit, on meeting Andy, I wasn't fully expecting things to work out. Andy seemed too good to be true; a dentist who owned his own home, a strong Christian involved heavily at church, and not to mention handsome. For the first three months of dating, I kept any details about my struggles private. When Andy learned about them, he just seemed to accept that side of me, not questioning over details, and not long after this he began talking with me about our future together.

Ironically, at our wedding the scripture shared was the passage from Ecclesiastes, which explains how 'Two are better than one ... if they fall, one will lift up his companion ... Though one may be overpowered by another, two can withstand him. And a threefold cord is not quickly broken' (Ecclesiastes 4:9,10,12, NKJV). Many believe the threefold cord refers to the unique strength in a marriage when Jesus is at the centre. We could not have predicted the poignancy of these words.

I have to say that Andy definitely set a precedent in the level of unconditional love and acceptance he showed to me in the first years of our marriage. Although initially my condition was stable, with the pressure of moving house in 2009, I became unwell and once again experienced an episode of depression. I will never forget how Andy offered me reassurance at that time to counteract my natural sense of insecurity. I know that this time wasn't easy for Andy, but he would often tell me that he wasn't fazed, and when he said his vows, 'for better or for worse, in sickness and in health', he fully accepted the level of support he may have to give me.

I admired how he was so pragmatic and didn't allow his own emotions to affect his commitment to do what he knew was right. I could learn so much from this example. The majority of my problems had been rooted in me being dictated to by my feelings. Andy's approach was indeed biblical; we are instructed in 2 Corinthians 5:7 to 'live by faith, not by sight', and this can also be interpreted to live by faith and not by feelings. Andy continues to abide by these principles and it is this resolve that has allowed him to remain mentally strong in the face of such harrowing physical disability. I again experienced an episode of being unwell in the year leading up to Andy's stroke, but this time it was much more severe and lasted several months. Andy was again impeccable in the love and support he offered.

So that is the background to the lead-up to the stroke. It goes without saying that when Andy's illness hit, people were concerned not only for Andy but also as to how I would cope. I am sure it was in answer to many people's prayers, but I straight away had a rich sense of comfort and strength.

Not long after the stroke, I was spending some time in prayer. I was reading the story in the Old Testament of the Israelites in the desert and how God promised to give them manna from heaven, not just as a one-off but as an ongoing sustenance whilst they were in the wilderness waiting to reach the Promised Land. I somehow felt distinctly that this new sense of courage wasn't just a result of the body's in-built fight or flight survival instinct, but that it was the start of an ongoing and lasting provision for my emotional healing.

Something that quickly became my lifeline was the Monday and Friday night prayer meetings at our church (the Friday night prayer had been started to pray specifically for Andy). I would arrive feeling emotionally frazzled, weary and anxious, which is the natural response to such a dire situation; however, I would always leave feeling encouraged and energised, ready to give spiritual comfort to Andy and generally be his cheerleader. Whenever there were setbacks, of which there were many, and when things seemed hopeless, I could always be certain that I would see things differently if I spent time at rest in God's presence.

There was a unique power that came from meeting with other Christians. The other women saw it as their ministry to pray each week for Andy's and my own specific needs. These times were like healing balm, where I regularly sensed afresh God's unconditional love and affirmation of me, and was able to let go of some of the fears which had previously fuelled my depression. God was not harsh and demanding, but tender and compassionate (Psalm 145:8), the lifter of my head (Psalm 3:3), longing to bear my burdens (1 Peter 5:7), giving me beauty for ashes and the oil of gladness instead of mourning (Isaiah 61:3).

The irony was that although on the outside my circumstance were as bleak as could be, my husband had Locked-in syndrome and all our hopes and plans seemed in tatters, I was somehow being carried throughout the ten months that Andy was in hospital, and knew a sense of courage, hope and peace amongst the storm.

In terms of Andy's healing and recovery, throughout the initial months, I shared his faith for a full restoration. Every new development was charted against the journeys of the other two once Locked-in sufferers, who had made a significant recovery and walked out of hospital: Kate Allatt in the UK, and Pete Coghlan in Australia. With all the prayer that was going up, coupled with Andy's determination, surely he could achieve a similar level of recovery?

To begin with, Andy's progress seemed to be competing, particularly in regards to his eating and his tracheostomy being removed. However, as time crept on, progress was becoming ever slower and Andy seemed to be losing ground, not meeting the recovery milestones we had all hoped for. I had concluded from Kate's and Pete's story that if you kept working hard, anything could be possible. The result was that I pushed Andy to work harder. I now think that maybe this was a bit too simplistic. Even though Kate and Pete had both initially been locked in, and so experienced identical symptoms to Andy, the effects of any stroke are unique to each individual, and so no two recoveries are comparable.

Another pressure that I initially felt was that perhaps I wasn't praying fervently enough and so I inevitably pushed myself to pray harder for Andy's healing. This approach makes the assumption that it is always God's will that we shouldn't have to suffer. I now, however, realise that I need to seek after God rather than seek after healing in and of itself. If, in my pursuit of God, He chooses to give me the gift of faith for a miraculous healing, then this is His prerogative, not mine. Ultimately, God is most interested in our own spiritual health and the lives of those to whom we minister because we are in these circumstances. I also feel that I am too close to the situation to pray for it sometimes, and it is then when we rely on the prayers of others. Throughout this process, I have had the faith for a gradual healing and seem to only have the capacity to focus my prayers on the next small stage of recovery. These prayer points have been updated on the blog: http://andydaviesupdate. blogspot.co.uk. Nevertheless, I have not given up on the faith I originally had and still believe that all things are possible according to God's will and perfect timing.

Chapter 16

Emma's Story: Part 2

When Andy came home from hospital, there were new challenges to face. Even though we were ten months' on, Andy still had no functional movement apart from the flicker in his right thumb, which he used to control his computer. He relied on the carer and myself for all his care needs: feeding, washing, manual handling, etc. Although Andy coming home was wonderful in one sense, and he was ecstatic to be out of hospital, the situation was still far from perfect. Andy continued to experience intense frustration, which is indeed understandable, but these outbursts were compounded by the effects of the stroke; it was, and still is, far from easy being on the receiving end, and we have had to learn how to relate to one another all over again. I have also found it difficult at times to adjust to having live-in carers and the dynamic that this also adds to our marriage.

Despite our difficulties, there have indeed been testimonies of God's sustaining comfort, not least in the fact that throughout the three years since Andy's stroke, I can honestly say that I am the healthiest that I have ever been emotionally. It is the longest period of time that I have not had an episode of major depression. On a day-to-day basis, I have been much freer in my thinking and in my ability to enjoy life. I am also still able to work, although it is very part-time hours. Wonderfully, my company kept my job open for me throughout the time Andy was first poorly. I find it really cathartic for us to still have interests that we do separately. Andy is able to use the time to work on university assignments with his study facilitator.

One of the things that we had been praying into more recently was Andy's ankles, and this has been one powerful way that we have experienced God ministering to us. During the time Andy was in an induced coma, the brain's swelling meant that the tendons in his ankles had significantly shortened. By the time Andy was out of intensive care, his feet were like a ballerina's.

Two and a half years on, and with all efforts to rectify the ankles non-surgically having been exhausted, we were finally told that an operation was our only option if we were to have any hope of Andy being able to stand. On various occasions, we kept coming back to the scripture in Psalm 18:36: 'You provide a broad path for my feet, so that my ankles do not give way.' We held on to this. However, our faith was shaken when Andy had his initial pre-op assessment to ensure he was physically fit to go ahead with the surgery. The surgeon measured the capillary refill time in both feet, but was alarmed by how poor Andy's circulation appeared to be; surgery would pose a significant threat of thrombosis or infection. We were both devastated, and were faced with the dilemma of whether we should proceed in the face of such grave risks. We spoke only with close family and Pastor Stuart, and after concluded that it would be unwise; we would have to relinquish any hopes of Andy standing, medically speaking.

Just weeks later, a letter arrived inviting us to be assessed by a vascular surgeon. It was also around this time that we attended a Christian youth camp for an evening; Stuart was ministering and we wanted to support him. Our friends Dan and Lianne were there.

Ironically, Lianne was part of Andy's first youth group when she was just fourteen. She subsequently stopped attending church, but rediscovered her faith in her early twenties when she began attending the small group that Andy and I were leading. Dan, her then boyfriend, didn't share Lianne's beliefs, but was supportive of her, and we got to know them both.

On the night of the actual stroke, Dan and Lianne were

with us for dinner, which was, of course, dramatically interrupted when Andy began experiencing the initial symptoms of the stroke and had to attend A&E. When Andy was still intubated, a prayer meeting was organised to pray for Andy, and I noticed that Dan was there. It was not long after this that Dan became a Christian, and later he and Lianne got married. How wonderful that in this youth meeting, nearly three years after Andy's stroke, Dan was now able to minister to us. After Stuart had finished preaching, Dan and Lianne approached us and asked if they could pray with Andy. As Dan was praying, he said that he had a mental image of 'a heart pumping really hard', making a 'whoosh whoosh' sound, but didn't know what it meant. Andy and I didn't talk about it afterwards, but I wondered whether it could be relevant to the operation.

Now, at the meeting with the vascular surgeon, an ultrasound scan was able to measure the blood flow in Andy's feet and ankles. As we heard the blood passing through each artery, we indeed heard the 'whoosh whoosh' sound that Dan had described just days earlier. The specialist then reassured us that Andy's circulation was as normal as you or I, so he could safely go ahead with the operation because any risks were now minimised. In November 2014, just four months ago at the time of writing, Andy had the operation. He has already been standing with remarkably less assistance and can now transfer from his recliner to his wheelchair without a hoist at home.

Of course, life is very different now to what either of us had planned or hoped for. People have often asked how I cope with the fact that having children might not be an option for us; it certainly doesn't seem possible at this present time. It is something that I have battled with, and it can be particularly difficult to watch friends and relatives be blessed with children. A time recently when I was particularly grappling with my desire to be a mother, I was comforted by one of the Hebrew names of God, detailed in Genesis 16:13, El Roi, which means 'the God who sees me'. Just reading that name was enough and I was overcome by a sense of joy and ability to continue in the state that I am for now. I have to accept this state. Between us, God has blessed us with four beautiful godchildren. It is an honour to have such a role, and I love spending time with each of them. Indeed, if am yearning for what I don't have at this moment in time, children of my own, I can miss this wonderful opportunity to be such a special part of each of their lives. I still, however, have not abandoned the hope of having children, but I have just yielded this desire to my loving heavenly Father, knowing that God still has good plans for us, whatever these may contain. When I speak of knowing that God has good plans for us, I am reminded of the scripture in Romans 8:28

where it says 'in all things God works for the good of those who love him, who have been called according to his purpose'. I think we could misunderstand the significance of this verse if we only applied it to our physical existence. Whenever I think of God blessing us, I have to exercise faith and accept that not everything will make sense in the here and now. I believe that God's ultimate goal for us is that we be more like Christ, and often the very means by which this happens is through us persevering in spite of very difficult circumstances; maybe this is why we are instructed to consider it pure joy when we face trials (James 1:2,3). I also know for certain that there will be a day where there will be no more tears and no more death, and God will wipe away my tears (Revelation 21:4; 7:17). In light of all this, as Christians we can know an unusual peace and joy in the midst of very difficult times, and often this can be a means through which others can see Christ in us. I definitely think that God is using us to support others in a way that we couldn't have done had it not been for the stroke.

One scripture that has been important to me more recently is Psalm 23 and the beautiful picture of God preparing a table for us in the presence of our enemies. This suggests that it is not always God's will to take away our difficulties, but for us to know his blessing in spite of them. In Psalm 110 there is a picture of us sitting down until God makes our enemies His footstool. This speaks of the rest and contentment we can still enjoy in surrendering what we can't control to God. Another scripture that has been key to me throughout this time is Psalm 103 where David instructs himself to 'Bless the LORD' (NKJV), perhaps despite his feelings and circumstances. There are so many things that are outside our control, but we all need to take responsibility to choose to bless the Lord, and recall all His benefits. If God never answered any of my prayers, He has still forgiven me completely, given me eternal life, and is healing me emotionally. If we are able to put our obvious difficulties aside for a moment, there are numerous benefits which we still enjoy.

We remain having to battle from day to day with the severe incapacity that Andy has been left with since the stroke, but blessings can come when, at times, we reach a low point and can't see a way through; somehow there is some small shaft of encouragement that lifts us.

I remember speaking to Barbara, Andy's mum, just a few days after Andy's stroke, and relaying what a wonderful husband he had been and the excellent support he had given me. She said something so profound – that over the course of a marriage the amount that each person puts into the marriage balances itself out, even if at times it can seem as if it's all one way. Although I have to support Andy in very obvious ways, Andy continues to support me. He is able to support us both financially, but he is also able to support me emotionally and I really value this. His support in this way, even since the stroke, has definitely contributed to the emotional stability that I now enjoy.

Chapter 17

Three Years On

- by Barbara

For you have been given the privilege of serving
Christ, not only by believing in him, but also by
suffering for him.
(Philippians 1:29, GNT)

When he wrote his letter to the Philippians, the
apostle Paul was in prison, chained, and under threat
of execution, but the letter to the church in Philippi is
full of hope and peace. Reading from the beginning of
the chapter, I was stunned to see the following verse,
highlighted and annotated by myself many times over
the past three years:

...being confident of this, that he who began a good
work in you will carry it on to completion until the day
of Christ Jesus. (Philippians 1:6)

The first time I heard this verse was when we were
staying with Andy in November 2012, a time when

he was depressed and wondering how he could carry on living, imprisoned in his own body. Andy's faithful friend, Ben, prayed the most beautiful prayer with the assurance that God would indeed complete the good work he had begun in Andy. It struck me then that despite the seemingly desperate situation in which Andy now languished his life (and ours), is God's work in progress in us. I didn't know at the time that those words were from the Bible, but the following Sunday, in our own church back in Burscough, the minister preached on this very verse! I can't remember what was preached, only that these words were for all those who have entrusted their lives to Jesus Christ and seek to serve him. Yet again the same verse appeared in my Bible-reading notes the very day my husband, Trevor, and I started an intensive nine-month-long course in Bible study and discipleship. To me, it is these incidents, that some may call coincidences, which reassure me that although we don't know why we are going through some desperate times, we can be sure that Christ is with us.

This, then, gave me the guidance and inspiration for my final contribution to this amazing book, painstakingly written by Andy over many months, each word either typed one letter at a time using the only physical control Andy has, head movement and a tiny flicker in his thumb, or dictated to Emma one word at a time as he uses naturally exhaled air from his lungs to speak. Andy cannot even take a voluntary breath.

I am absolutely convinced that God is in complete control, that He has a great divine plan for all of humanity, and personally I feel wonderfully privileged that He has called me to be part of the incredible things He is doing in the lives of those I love.

The life-changing effects of Andy's stroke have had a deeply profound effect on all who know and love him, but also on many people around the world who have been moved to pray, help and support Andy, Emma and all the family. Andy's progress has been posted on a blog which has been copied and forwarded to many others who have no internet access. This book is the culmination of many months' work to bring Andy and Emma's story to an even wider audience.

Although outwardly Andy's physical rehabilitation is barely perceptible, his achievements are truly amazing. His core strength and stamina has improved to enable him to sit in a wheelchair for up to twelve hours a day, attending lectures at college and travelling long distances by car and public transport. He continues to keep his limbs supple with neuro-physiotherapy, hydrotherapy and exercise at home each week. Of course we, his loved ones, had our own hopes and prayers for healing in specific areas but while he was still in hospital, Andy told me he could cope with the inability to walk as long as he could talk. His greatest desire was to be able to communicate with family, friends and carers. This was his main goal, and we are now seeing this achieved most wonderfully in so many ways; I am reminded of the prayer of Paul to the Ephesians where he writes:

And I pray that you ... grasp how wide and long and high and deep is the love of Christ, and ... know this love that surpasses knowledge ... Now to him who is able to do immeasurably more than all we ask or imagine, according to his power that is at work within us, to him be glory in the church and in Christ Jesus throughout all generations, for ever and ever! Amen. (Ephesians 3:17–21)

These verses have repeatedly been given to me since November 2011, and make me pause to reflect on all the prayers for Andy's healing and the return of functional movement in his arms and legs. Some prayers are for standing and walking, and some for the use of his hands.

We long for Andy to be as he was before, skilfully making, doing and active. But the verses above have shown me time and again that God's love for us is far beyond our poor understanding, and that our prayer requests are woefully limiting God's power because He can do so much more than our wildest imagining.

So, looking back, we can see God has given Andy the

necessary skills to talk once more, chat with family and friends at home, and use the internet to make video phone calls. He can discuss and dictate assignments for his theology course and has written this book. That is some serious communication!

The powerful messages we were given during the latter days Andy spent in rehab, waiting to go home for good, were our reassurance from God that although life we had classed as 'normal' was no more, He would strengthen and guide us into a 'new normal' life. We have often talked about 'our new normal' since that horrific day, 1 November 2011, when doctors could give us no hope. Andy and Emma's life together, as they had known it, had been turned upside down; all their plans, hopes and dreams were shattered, and they faced a bleak, uncertain future.

We, their family and friends, were left bewildered and hurting, knowing that all our lives had changed forever. We all had to learn to walk this path of the 'new normal', trusting that God would lead us, guide us and protect us; we had to put all our faith in God because there was no human skill, medicine or technology which could save, heal and restore Andy. We who love Andy had nowhere to turn, no one who could help us deal with this devastating, life-changing disaster. So we turned to God. So numb we were unable to pray ourselves, we simply sent out requests by phone, email and social media: 'PLEASE PRAY FOR ANDY.'

What followed was the most powerful outpouring of God's love. We were all filled with His presence and given the courage, strength and faith to support Andy and Emma through this nightmare. For me personally, it was the words of favourite songs and hymns which became prayers in those terrifying early days. To me, the words I heard and sang to Andy as he fought for his life were a precious gift of reassurance and peace from God, His prayer to me. Within six days Andy was moved out of Critical Care – he was alive, out of immediate danger, and he had a future reinforced with these words:

'For I know the plans I have for you,' declares the LORD, 'plans to prosper you and not to harm you, plans to give you hope and a future.' (Jeremiah 29:11)

The LORD himself goes before you and will be with you; he will never leave you nor forsake you. (Deuteronomy 31:8)

Looking back over these past three years, it is truly awesome to see how God has showered us with so many blessings; out of what seemed to be the most appalling tragedy has come 'immeasurably more than all we ask or imagine' (Ephesians 3:20). In those dark November days when we prayed that Andy would live, we could never have imagined all that God had planned for us for the future, or how much blessing would be poured on us. There have been many painful, frightening and dark paths to walk, but when we have been sinking into depths of despair we have been reassured and strengthened, blessed in so many ways. The words of hymns and songs, the goodwill messages of friends, have all been sources of blessing and encouragement, but God's blessings of love and hope have very often come directly from Him, written thousands of years ago in the Bible. It is no coincidence that on a particular day in a particular situation we are so often directed to a verse of scripture which meets our specific needs, questions or doubts.

The day Andy was admitted to hospital, the following verses were the subject of my Bible-reading notes and on that day I knew that God was speaking to me, preparing me for what was to come and reassuring me that Andy would be well. The same verses were written in a card from a dear friend of Andy's which arrived a few days later.

Even youths grow tired and weary, and young men stumble and fall; but those who hope in the Lord will renew their strength. They will soar on wings like eagles; they will run and not grow weary, they will walk and not be faint. (Isaiah 40:30,31)

At that time the message of hope was just what I needed to keep me strong and faithful, firmly believing that Andy would indeed regain his strength, walk and run again. I firmly believed this promise and it gave me the faith and determination to help Andy and Emma through this nightmare. As the months and years have passed, my faith has not diminished that the Lord is indeed healing and renewing, not only Andy but all of us. So why isn't Andy able to walk and run or even move his legs? The answer came repeatedly: 'God's timing is perfect.' In due course, another verse about eagle's wings was the subject of my daily readings:

He [God] was like an eagle hovering over its nest, overshadowing its young, then spreading its wings, lifting them into the air, teaching them to fly. (Deuteronomy 32:11, The Message)

The explanation of this passage answered my questions. Eagle's nests are often built high up in tall trees or rocky crags. When the eagle chicks are fully fledged and need to leave the nest, the mother eagle begins to demolish the nest and nudge them out, forcing them to try their wings. They manage a few flaps and their little wings quickly tire, but father eagle is already in place, underneath, ready to catch the falling chick on his wings and teach it to fly. What a wonderful analogy! When we face terrifying situations in which we have no strength, skills or resources with which to save ourselves, we have no option but to trust our Father. Just as the parent eagle lifts its young on wings and soars in the air, so we must learn to trust in God's unfailing love, protection and guidance. We may or may not see Andy walking again, but I am convinced that God is in control of Andy's life and ours, catching us as we fall, lifting us up and teaching us to 'fly' as we trust in Him.

And I pray that you, being rooted and established in love, may have power, together with all the saints, to grasp how wide and long and high and deep is the love of Christ, and to know this love that surpasses knowledge – that you may be filled to the measure of all the fullness of God. Now to him who is able to do immeasurably more than all we ask or imagine, according to his power that is at work within us, to him be glory in the church and in Christ Jesus throughout all generations, for ever and ever! Amen. (Ephesians 3:17–21 NIV 1984)